W9-CEM-228

The Uninvited

To Write to the Author

If you wish to contact the author or would like more information about this book, please write to the author in care of Llewellyn Worldwide and we will forward your request. Both the author and publisher appreciate hearing from you and learning of your enjoyment of this book and how it has helped you. Llewellyn Worldwide cannot guarantee that every letter written to the author can be answered, but all will be forwarded. Please write to:

Steven LaChance
℅ Llewellyn Worldwide
2143 Wooddale Drive, Dept. 978-0-7387-1357-1
Woodbury, MN 55125-2989, U.S.A.

Please enclose a self-addressed stamped envelope for reply, or $1.00 to cover costs. If outside the U.S.A., enclose an international postal reply coupon.

Many of Llewellyn's authors have websites with additional information and resources. For more information, please visit our website at http://www.llewellyn.com.

THE
UNINVITED

Llewellyn Publications
Woodbury, Minnesota

The Uninvited: The True Story of the Union Screaming House © 2008 by Steven LaChance. All rights reserved. No part of this book may be used or reproduced in any manner whatsoever, including Internet usage, without written permission from Llewellyn Publications except in the case of brief quotations embodied in critical articles and reviews.

First Edition
First Printing, 2008

Book design by Steffani Sawyer
Cover art ©2008 Colin Anderson/Blend Images/Punchstock
Cover design by Ellen Dahl
Editing by Brett Fechheimer
Llewellyn is a registered trademark of Llewellyn Worldwide, Ltd.

Library of Congress Cataloging-in-Publication Data

LaChance, Steven, 1965–
  The uninvited : the true story of the Union screaming house / Steven
LaChance.—1st ed.
     p. cm.
  ISBN 978-0-7387-1357-1
1. Haunted houses—Missouri—Union. 2. Demoniac
possession—Missouri—Union. 3. LaChance, Steven, 1965– 4. LaChance,
Steven, 1965– —Family. 5. Union (Mo.)—Biography. I. Title.
  BF1472.U6L33 2008
  133.1'2977863—dc22
                                                        2008024235

Llewellyn Worldwide does not participate in, endorse, or have any authority or responsibility concerning private business transactions between our authors and the public.
  All mail addressed to the author is forwarded but the publisher cannot, unless specifically instructed by the author, give out an address or phone number.
  Any Internet references contained in this work are current at publication time, but the publisher cannot guarantee that a specific location will continue to be maintained. Please refer to the publisher's website for links to authors' websites and other sources.

Llewellyn Publications
A Division of Llewellyn Worldwide, Ltd.
2143 Wooddale Drive, Dept. 978-0-7387-1357-1
Woodbury, Minnesota 55125-2989, U.S.A.
www.llewellyn.com

Printed in the United States of America

Thank you to all of you for standing by me through the darkest of days and the most horrific of hours:

My three children
My mom and dad
My brothers, their wives
My sister, whom I miss daily
Denice Jones, my paranormal sister
John Zaffis, my guide
Dr. Jimmy Lowery
Carmen Reed, fellow survivor
Theresa and Mike Reavey
Tim Yancey
Tim Clifton
Karen Stratman
Keith Age
The Booth brothers
Father Mark
Betsy Belanger
Cari Stone
The *Ghostly Talk* guys, Scott and Doug
Madame Star
Tracey Guitar
Anni Swierk
All of those who weren't afraid to let me tell my story!

Contents

Preface

Are you alone?
Are you sure?

Alone—I used to think I understood the meaning of that word. That was a long time ago. Years ago. Alone for me now does not have the same meaning.

What if I told you that there is a good possibility that you are never alone?

Are you looking over your shoulder right now? If not, maybe you should be.

Did you ever have that feeling when you are taking a shower that there is someone hiding, waiting, breathing just on the other side of the shower curtain? You see the curtain begin to move slowly in and out. Were you alone then? Or was that just a little lie that you told yourself to make yourself feel better? To make it easier to cope with whatever was lurking on that other side of that curtain.

Have you ever sat in your living room at night in your favorite chair, maybe reading your favorite book, maybe like you are doing right now, and felt as though someone was watching you? Or maybe breathing down the back of your neck? Sometimes you might think you see something moving out of the corner of your eye. Did you tell yourself it was your imagination? Was that a rationalization to keep yourself from running out the front door, screaming?

Have you ever been in your bed at night, lights out, just about to fall asleep, when you hear a shuffle on the carpet at the end of your bed? Maybe you sit up with the understanding, for one split second, that the darkness moves. Did you sit there frozen for that moment in fear? Afraid to move. How many times have you told yourself that it must be your eyes playing tricks on you? A trick of the light or a moving car casting a shadow as it drove down the street? But then you remember that you didn't hear the sound of a car.

I have told myself many things in all of the instances described above. Deceiving myself, like you, that I was truly alone. Yes, I was once like you. I used to let my mind explain away many things that should not have been explained away. But now I know the truth. And soon you will, too.

You aren't alone. At any given time, in any given place, there could be something lurking just to the right or left out of the corner of your eye. Open your eyes and you can see them. Open your eyes and watch the darkness move before you. Leave the rationalizations behind you, for just a little while.

Yes, I was once like you. Lying to myself. Fooling myself. Convincing myself that I could be truly alone whenever I wanted to be. Now I know the truth. Security is a state of mind and this story, my story, is going to pull that blanket right out from under you. This is a true story. I know, because it happened to me.

Are you alone? Are you sure? Maybe you should turn on a few more lights.

Prologue

This story has been told a thousand times before, passed down from generation to generation; it's a cautionary tale for those who care to listen and heed its message. It's a trap for those who choose to ignore it or who forget it. Just how do I persuade you to listen to a story that's been told so many times? How do I find a way to make it ring true and honest for a new generation? The story carries truth, it carries a warning, and it's a rite of passage that everyone must hear. Oh, the circumstances may be slightly different from the stories that came before, but the meat is still there, bare flesh flayed from the bone by someone or something unknown and unseen.

Some will call this a tale, an old wives' tale, campfire lore intended to frighten young children and amuse grownups who were once scared little kids themselves. Even if this were an old wives' tale or merely a modern metaphor for evil, the warning is, and always will be, the same: there isn't always a logical explanation for things that happen. And the unexplainable can be a trap for the family that's unaware of the complexities of the unknown, for it casts a spell and sweeps everyone into its vortex as quickly as a man snaps his fingers. And even when the writing is on the proverbial wall, drawn in blood— deep, dark, fresh blood—the warning signs are still ignored. *Ignored!* How foolish is the man or woman who believes that he or she controls everything between heaven and hell. The great American dream can quickly morph into a nightmare for those unwilling to see and heed the warning signs of the unexplainable.

* * *

The nightmare is always the same: the darkness, the sounds, the stairs, and the fear . . . always the same fear. If only it played out differently, if only it became a story with a beginning, a middle, and an end. But no; the nightmare always picks up right in the middle. It leaves behind its unforgettable details along with my screams, which inevitably follow the dream each time it revisits me in my sleep.

It's dark. I'm standing on the basement steps. They're old, wooden, creaky, and worn. Flowered, neon-print wallpaper is peeling off the walls of the stairway. Bright flowers of seventies orange and yellow with huge leaves of olive green are dimly visible in the moonlight cast through the basement windows below. I grasp the handrail and steady myself, calming my nerves before beginning my slow decent into the moonlit darkness below. The stairs seem to go on forever; they seem to extend way beyond into the darkness, with something foreboding waiting below. With each step I take, the creaking of the stairs announces my progress to whatever lurks in the shadows.

I hear water running in the basement, and I am going to investigate its origin. A few more steps farther into the mouth of darkness and I see a candle burning. It emits a warm glow. There is an unattended lit candle in the basement . . . I easily dismiss it from my mind and turn my attention to the sound of the rushing water. Along with the water I now hear breathing, the labored breathing of a man; he sounds excited, almost sexually excited. I turn back toward the candlelight, and I can see that the water is coming from the butcher shower. A man stands beneath it, his back to me, his figure revealed by the candlelight in the otherwise dark basement.

The water and the man's breathing echo throughout the base-ment; he still hasn't sensed my presence. I watch as he tries to cleanse himself, purifying himself of a dark substance, scrubbing his already raw skin. Even as I watch him, his labored breathing becomes panicked and so does the pace of his scrubbing. Whatever he is trying to wash away has thoroughly stained him. He can't get clean!

He turns; I can see his frontal torso in the light. It's covered in blood. Is he looking at me? I can't tell, but I sense his evil eyes sweep across me as he continues washing.

The room begins to spin. The sound of his desperation matches the tempo of his hands scrubbing his body. The room keeps spinning and spinning. I still feel his eyes on me. I can't breathe. Oh my God, I can't breathe . . .

PART 1

THE
INVITATION

1

How did I end up in Union, Missouri, in the first place? I'd always been attracted to big cities, and during my youth I can remember fooling myself that I'd actually get the hell out of here. That never happened. Through the years Union became the place I called home. Once you've put your roots down, it's very hard to pull them up to move on. Union is where my roots are. This is home.

Union, Missouri is a small town fifty miles southwest of St. Louis. Take Interstate 44 west of the city, and the St. Louis suburbs quickly give way to smaller communities. Union is one of those small rural communities—far enough away from the city to avoid the crowds, noise, and confusion. Pollution in Union has never been a problem. Look up at the sky on any clear night, and you'll see stars so clear and bright that it's sometimes hard to believe they're real. Union is a rural town, a small town. Like the town itself, its residents have aged. These days a small farming community like Union isn't booming, nor is it wealthy. But nor would I say the people in Union are for the most part poor; they just know how to make do. Generations of families on top of generations. The family trees of long-time Union residents are as long and wide as the streets in the old part of town. Union is the county seat of Franklin County, and the town square with its huge old courthouse acts as the centerpiece of town. The courthouse is rumored to have seen many hangings in its day. Old folks talk about families packing up picnic lunches to eat while sitting outside the courthouse, watching the bodies as they fell and went limp on their nooses.

The true history of a town like Union is always kept by the old. And Union has its secrets, just like any other small town. Historic? Of course it is, but you would never know of the history and battles that it's seen because most of the historic locations remain unmarked. Union, Missouri is a small town like any other, and I call it my home. I live here and I raised my children here. It's the place I've worked, sang, and prayed. It's my home. For better or worse, this is where I've laid down my roots. This is my home.

*   *   *

I wish I could claim that I've led a fairy-tale existence in which good always conquers evil. Who wouldn't want that kind of life? Mine began that way, I thought. I had a happy childhood. I was born on January 3, 1965, in a hospital in St. Louis. Born to devout Lutheran parents, I was a large baby, twenty-four inches long. I spent my early years living in St. Louis County, in the city's northern suburbs. When I was eleven, my parents decided to leave St. Louis behind and move to the country, to Franklin County. As a city boy I always felt somewhat out of place in a farming community. We lived between the two towns of Washington and Union, right outside the small township of Krakow. My parents still live there, while I now live in Union.

I was a good student, with high grades and even higher expectations. I was a great speaker and a fair musician. College was successful, and I made my mark as a national-champion debater. I married at twenty-three and became a first-time father shortly thereafter, when Lydia, my daughter, was born.

Lydia came into this world as a crying, screaming bundle in September 1988. Her mother's pregnancy had been uneventful, and the delivering physician had no reason to suspect that Lydia's birth would be anything but routine. That quickly changed after my wife went into labor. Lydia, as if sensing the events that would one day shake our family to its foundation, poked her tiny head into the world and immediately returned to her mother's womb. The mood in the delivery room changed from one of relaxed if anxious anticipation to one of controlled chaos. Lydia turned when she elected to postpone her birth, and she was now in a breech position. Both her mother's and Lydia's vital signs indicated they were in distress. Suddenly, I was in danger of losing them both. An emergency cesarean section was performed, however, and Lydia was finally placed in my arms. Her tears and tiny form brought me out of the depths of my worry. Little did I know that Lydia's birth was a true harbinger of her personality and events that I would never have been able to imagine. Throughout the years she would always walk to the beat of her own drum. Strong-willed and levelheaded: that is my Lydia.

A year later my son Michael was born—one year and six days later to be exact. His birth went off without a hitch.

"Mr. LaChance?"

My attention was drawn away from my wife who was still positioned on the birthing table as if the hurried medical staff intended to crucify her later. Michael was brought into this world to the sound of his parents laughing, a sound he wouldn't hear for long.

"Mr. LaChance? I'd like to introduce you to your son."

The nurse handed me the most serious little baby I'd ever seen. *Serious* would continue to be the best word to describe Michael as he grew up. He was born amidst laughter and optimism on the part of his parents, but a pessimist he would be. Serious, with a deep sincerity. That is my Michael.

Matthew was born eighteen months later, in January 1991, during one of the coldest winters on record. His was a natural birth, not as dramatic as Lydia's and not nearly as optimistic as Michael's. For reasons only she might understand, the light had already gone out in his mother's eyes. Despite being born on the coldest day of the century, even as a newborn Matthew was the warmest and sweetest of children, full of energy and life. But the first time I held him in my arms, this little bundle of energy calmed down at the sound of my voice.

"Hello, little man," I whispered softly. And he was a "little man." His birth weight was ten pounds, and he was over twenty-four inches long. From then on he would always be taller than other children, a force to be reckoned with and one that couldn't be ignored. Inside his oversized body was a heart that would always overflow with love and affection as he matured. Oh, yes, a sweet and gentle soul was born into my life that day, and my heart was as warm as the day was cold. A gentle giant with a heart of gold: that is my Matthew.

And they lived happily ever after—how I wish I could conclude the story of my children's births that way. Unfortunately, Matthew's birth would be the last happy day in the life of my marriage. Four years after Matthew's arrival, I came home to find my wife sullen and depressed. Her dull eyes beseeched me to understand as she struggled to say her next words: "I'm leaving you."

It's funny, but when you are in the midst of living your life, you become blind to the truth that's right in front of you. I hadn't seen this coming. And even if I had, I would have ignored it or talked myself out of it. It's hard to see the writing on the proverbial wall when you are constantly trying to hide from it.

"It's not that I want to divorce you," she continued, trying to reassure me with a voice that I already mistrusted. "I want to divorce the children." She stood to cross the room. "Dammit, Steven, I never wanted to be a mother. I did that for you. You always knew you wanted to be a father. It was and is just not for me. I can't do it. I try and I try, but I just can't seem to do it. This is the right thing. This is the most right thing that I can do for them and for you. It's me. It isn't you and it isn't them. This is about me." She steadied herself for what she had to say to me next. "You have until Friday for you and the kids to find someplace to live. I haven't paid the rent in six months. Tomorrow they're turning off the electricity." At that moment, I began to gain the full, horrible understanding of what was happening. She was not only leaving us, but she was also stealing the money that was meant to keep us secure, keep us alive. She was leaving us homeless.

The words echoed in my befuddled mind, and by the time I could think again, she was gone. Where had I failed? What had I done to lead her to leave us so abruptly? Why like this? Without a home. With only the shirts on our backs and very little that we could take with us. Just enough that each person could put into a box and bag of their own. So many things lost. Things that could never be replaced. A trust that was more than shattered.

Shocked and shaken, I tried to figure out what I would do next. What would I tell my children? How could I tell them that their mother had left them? They didn't ask for this. The only consolation I could summon up was that she had waited for me to return home. Through my daze I remember her saying that she had considered simply leaving them at the grocery store. Somebody, she had said, would have found them and contacted me. I couldn't imagine that the woman I had met, loved, married, and conceived a family with, the mother of my children, would have ever considered abandoning her children in such a heartless manner. They would never have recovered from a trauma like that.

The kids and I moved in with my parents for a six-month crash course in Parenting Skills 101. The women in my life, my mother and my wife, had allowed me to live a very sheltered life, and I had to learn even the simplest domestic skills. But I kept my eyes firmly on my children and the long road before us that we would have to travel together. Together? Who was I kidding? Although my parents would help as much as they could, ultimately I would have to do this alone, a single father to three young children. I certainly hadn't scripted this into my life plan. Life as I knew it had been dramatically, drastically, and permanently altered with a few words and the slamming of a door.

I would find in the coming months and years that I could manage a pretty good life for all of us. My wife's visits to her children became less and less frequent, and the children's desire to be with her diminished with the passage of time. Their wounds would be with them forever, but I did my best to bandage and soothe them. By the grace of God I hoped that in the coming years they would become mature adults secure in the knowledge that they were loved, even if they had been abandoned by their mother. I knew, though, that despite my best efforts, pain this deep and personal would leave them scarred. I was saddened every time I thought about it—saddened, pained, and hurt.

In the years to come I would try to figure out why it all went so wrong so fast. I never did find the answer for myself, for my children, or for her. What causes a mother to give up her young? That completely goes against the laws of nature. Was it a prolonged postpartum depression? A nervous breakdown? Or did she just simply lose her mind? I don't think I'll ever fully have the answer. At least she knew what was best for them. Her words still echo in my mind, even now, this many years later: "This is the most right thing that I can do for them and for you." Well, at least she got that much right.

2

Janice, my sister, died two years before my wife left us. The words were too hard for me to utter and too painful to comprehend. My sister was too young, too smart, and too full of life to die. She was my best friend, and I loved her. "Someday," she once said, "we'll be old, sitting on this porch watching our grandchildren play. That will be a wonderful day." Her words are still etched in my mind, and each day that passes reminds me of the curse of the living, those that are left behind to remember and mourn.

My sister had three beautiful girls, and she wasn't only a mother, she was aunt to my children and another nephew. She was my parents' only daughter and a sister to four brothers. How could this void be filled? I still don't have an answer for that.

Janice was three years older than I am, a fact she always enjoyed rubbing in. Once we both left home, we had weekly phone calls. No matter where we were or how busy life was, we found time to talk to each other. The calls could last for two hours or more. Amazingly, just when we felt we had said everything there was to say, we would find one more thing to keep the conversation going. Sometimes we would remember moments from our past. "Remember when I was five, and I had to have my tonsils taken out?" That was one of her favorite stories. "Remember how much you missed me? You slept with my pink sweater like it was a blanket." Of course I remembered. I miss her right now as I write this. The story of the pink sweater used to embarrass me, but now it is one of my favorites.

The last time I saw Janice alive was on Easter, a little less than a month before she died; we were all at our parents' house. Janice and I had been engaged in an ongoing argument, one that only siblings can have. She didn't like my wife, and she wasn't happy with the direction my life was headed. I didn't appreciate her comments and, considering that she was married to her third husband, I didn't think she was in a position to offer advice.

I didn't understand it at the time, but I realized later that she wanted more for me than what life had given to her. She didn't want me to make the same mistakes. Ultimately, none of it mattered on what would turn out to be our last day together.

After dinner I watched my mother and my sister wash the dishes. Our family was quite large so there were a lot of dishes. Mom, the cleanest woman on earth, always insisted she didn't want a dishwasher. "They simply don't get the dishes clean," she would tell us as we whined about helping her. That Easter evening, though, I realized Mom's insistence that her children help her do the dishes by hand had nothing to do with cleanliness; this had been her way of making sure she had time each day to talk to us. Now that we were adults, it was her way of catching up with us since our last visit home.

When the dishes were done, I stood up to go check on the kids who were playing in the large backyard of my youth. Suddenly, Janice turned from the sink and looked at me. Her eyes locked with mine, and then she hugged me and said, "You know I love you, don't you?" I still wonder why she chose that moment, on that day, to express her sibling affection, but it doesn't matter, for that memory has carried me through some of the darkest days of my life, and I will gratefully carry that memory to my grave. Whenever the grief became too much to handle, I could feel that hug from memory.

She died on a Monday in May, just a few weeks after Easter. My telephone rang; answering it, I thought it was my mother but I couldn't be certain. "Steven?" It sounded like my mother's voice, but there was something different about it. "Steven, Janice is dead." Dead? The walls and the world closed in on me. Grief ripped through my body and claimed it.

My mother's words echoed in my head as I drifted in and out of a fog of memories. "Steven! If you tell Mom, I'll play that tape of you cursing . . . I'm getting married, Steven . . . I'm getting the hell out of here . . . I had a miscarriage today; will you come over? . . . I think I'm pregnant . . . Being a mom is the coolest thing in the world! . . . Are you sure you want to marry her? I'm so proud of you. Now, don't go and fuck up your life."

Over and over memories of Janice came and went, mixed in with the nightmare of what lay before me: the horror on my father's face as he was given the news; my mother trying to remain composed despite the anguish that was clearly in her eyes; my father's hand calmly touching my shoulder, steadying me at the moment my knees gave way at the viewing. "Oh, no you don't," he said, his words penetrating the fog that had continued to engulf me. "If you think about this too much, it will drive you crazy."

My sister was dead. I could cite the medical reports of the physicians' theories behind her death, but it wouldn't change the outcome. Janice was dead.

"Remember when I used to tell you that I was going to throw myself in the sewer, and you would never see me again?" Her playful voice narrated the black-and-white memory that my mind replayed day and night, even seeping into my sleep. Awake or dreaming I could see us so plainly, two children peering into the oversized sewer, me crying because I didn't want her to go. Even after we grew up, my eyes teared up when I thought about that day. It doesn't take much for me to become the little boy listening to his taunting and laughing big sister. It's funny how a moment like that can paint the future. Janice and I, two children, two souls, lost in a sewer.

Her funeral was amazing. Cars lined up for miles in the procession to the little country cemetery, accompanying her to her final resting spot.

The fog of grief that had continued to engulf me lifted here and there. I have only brief snapshot-quality memories of that day. The strongest is of my daughter Lydia walking up to the grave and throwing a pink rose into my sister's grave. Instead of finding comfort in her sweet gesture, I found anger, pain, and fear. *This isn't how our lives were supposed to be. Janice and I were supposed to grow old together, watch our kids grow up together. We were supposed to be together watching over our children until they had children and grandchildren of their own.* The thought of Janice dead slapped me in the face over and over again; every time I thought about it, it was as if I were hearing the news for the first time.

Anger grew second by second, minute by minute. *Okay, God, why? You tell me why you did this. Why Janice? Why not some trashy, drugged-up junkie with nothing to contribute to society?* It didn't make any damned sense. I wanted to scream at him, I really did. I wanted to scream at him, *WHY?* But every time I tried, I would choke the sound back and push it into the deep recesses of my soul. And every time I swallowed my anger, my soul died a little. I could feel the quality of life being sucked out of me with every wave of angered emotion.

Pray, I was told. Oh, I prayed all right. That wasn't a problem, but my prayers were that I could take back every prayer I had ever uttered and erase from eternity every praise I had given up to him. *God of love? Show me!* He didn't love me and I hated him. My sister had lived, my sister had died. And I was left changed forever.

I wanted to die, but I couldn't. I still had my three children to raise, and Janice's three daughters to console. So, if I couldn't die, I could live a life full of anger and hatred toward God. *What "lesson" did God want us to learn from Janice's early death? There was nothing to be gained from her dying so young. And what did God propose that I tell her children? What reason could I give them that would satisfactorily explain why their mother was never coming home again? There is no logical way to explain why a seemingly healthy young woman could lie down for a nap on a sunny afternoon and not wake up. God, why didn't my sister wake up?*

Janice's youngest child had been playing in the next room. How could she know that her mommy lay dying in the next? When Janice's two older daughters came home, they continued to let her "nap." It was Janice's husband who found her when he came home from work. *How would the girls heal once they realized that they played while their mother lay dead in another room? What was the point to all of this?*

If a molecule of good came out of Janice's death, it was a new attitude for me; live for today because dead is dead. *Live the good life, baby, because once we're gone, we're gone. We are born here, we live here, we die here, and poof, lights out. Game called on account of DEAD.* Janice was dead and I had to move on.

With time my anger at God lessened, and over time I became at best agnostic, and at worst an atheist. If there were a God and an afterlife, God surely would have let Janice send me some sort of message of comfort. Of course I had no way of knowing the price I would eventually pay for turning my back to God, the price I would pay for my anger. An anger that slowly began to eat away at my spirit. An anger that would take me down the darkest of roads.

Early one morning about a year after Janice's death, Lydia told me she had seen Aunt Jan. "She was in my closet last night wearing a pretty yellow dress."

I kept my response even and measured as I told her that she had been dreaming.

"No, Daddy. She was there. She was in my closet. She told me to keep it a secret because you wouldn't understand."

My daughter was right. I didn't understand, at least not then.

3

Life is complex enough when a guy is on his own, but I had myself and three children to care for. Finding good housing for all of us was nearly impossible. First, I needed three bedrooms. Things would have been different if all my children were the same sex, but I had a mixed bag of kids. It was a blessed mixed bag but still one that posed some challenges for me. Early on, I found that landlords were willing to rent to me and my daughter, but if they also saw the two boys, the deal was over. For that reason, Lydia and I would go to any viewings and leave the boys with my parents. This system seemed to work. As long as the landlords didn't see the boys beforehand, it was easy to strike a bargain. I guess the sight of the entire brooding clan was too much for the average landlord.

Our first home was a two-bedroom apartment with a large bedroom that we could section off. The apartment complex itself was a rowdy place. The landlord's daughter and her boyfriend lived directly above us. When they weren't engaged in their weekly drunken fight, she would have her ear firmly glued to the floor, listening for any rule infractions on our part. After the second year, it became clear that we were growing out of this apartment.

We were thrilled that our second home was a real house, a little house situated on a quiet street in Union. Its owner had lived there from the time it was built until her death. We loved the hardwood floors; the kitchen was the house's largest room. But we lived in this house just one year. The landlord's cousins' house was adjacent to our backyard, and they were true hillbillies. The only time they did their laundry was when it rained; then they hung their clothes out on a line to wash. We never discovered how they survived in the winter. The hillbilly clan included a peeping Tom, whom my mother discovered spying in our windows while I was at work and she was staying with the children. When I caught up with him, I threatened to remove his manhood if he ever peeked in our windows again. In the meantime we began searching for a new place to live.

During this period I experienced my first paranormal event. The kids were at my parents' house, and I was getting ready for a long-deserved night out with some friends. I didn't notice anything unusual when I first came home, but after I took a shower I wrapped a towel around my waist to avoid my perverted neighbor's spying eyes and headed to the kitchen for a drink of water. What I saw caused me to pause in surprise. Every cabinet door in the kitchen was standing wide open. Shaking my head and muttering, I closed each door. The kids were being lazy, or they were trying to play a trick on me. I suspected a trick.

After we had moved in, we learned that the woman who had lived in the house before us had been dead for four days before someone found her lying in the middle of the kitchen. I briefly recalled that bit of knowledge as I closed the doors. Were we in a haunted house? I knew I was living in a house "haunted" by kids trying to pull a fast one on their old man. Unless I actually saw the dead woman's ghost opening the doors, I told the kids later, I was going to chalk this up to them playing a prank on me or a frantic search by one of them looking for something to eat. As far as I was concerned, that was the end of the story.

Our next home was another apartment. It had sloping ceilings, three bedrooms, and a balcony that looked out onto the hills. We lived on the second floor of a two-story building. Like our first apartment, this one was filled with loud and obnoxious neighbors. A group of college boys lived on the first floor. They liked to smoke pot, and its sweet, sickening odor would fill the building. For two years we lived with weekend parties and a neighbor below us who would bang on her ceiling every time we walked across the floor.

The landlady was worse. She was nosy, annoying, arrogant, and had no regard for her tenants' personal rights or feelings. As the owner, she felt it was within her rights to conduct inspections. During these "inspections," she would come into our home and go through all of our belongings. She wasn't inspecting for structural items that needed repairing, nor for leaky faucets or termites. Oh, no. She was "checking the condition of the drawers," and then carefully examining everything inside. "Let me see if this closet door is functioning properly," she would say, opening the door and studying the closet's contents before closing the door and leaving the room. No maintenance was ever performed on our apartment after these inspections; the only outcome was the invasion of our privacy. The only good thing about that apartment was the hill we lived on top of. That location saved us during the flood of 2000.

The flood came the night of May 6. The rain poured like I had never seen rain pour before. It sounded like nails were hitting the roof of the apartment, and it looked as though hell had come to the small town of Union. Throughout the night there were reports of stray propane tanks floating in the angry currents. People were dying out there, and we were stuck in the middle of it—waiting to see what more the weather could bring us, waiting to see if our home would be the next one hit by lightning, or worse, blown up by an errant propane tank.

With dawn the rain diminished. By mid-morning the water began to recede; by late afternoon it was completely gone. The only evidence of the storm's angry flight through town was the debris it had left in its wake.

When it was over, many people were homeless. Who would have guessed that the small Flat Creek that ran through the center of Union could become a raging river, destroying everything in its path? The images were chilling. The chaos was unimaginable. Questions danced through my brain. How long would we be cut off? How long would our utilities stay on? How long before the tap water would become undrinkable? Was our building still safe?

A state of emergency was declared, and Union was put under a curfew. Roadblocks were set up to keep people out of the worst-hit areas. It's a severe wake-up call for a community when armed guards block the roadways, demanding to see identification and know the purpose for each trip. It took nearly two years and millions of dollars for the damage to be cleaned up and repaired.

We had survived. The water had surrounded us, but we were safe on top of the hill. An island in the middle of the debris.

Anyone living in Union then will never forget that night, the night the waters raged.

4

I started a new job in May of that year, and it appeared that good luck would finally smile down upon the LaChance family. The job was with a photography company. I had already worked six years for studios located in major department stores. Now I had been hired to open a new studio by July in one of the biggest malls in St. Louis. The job was great: double the wages I used to make, better benefits, and the backing of one of America's largest corporations.

There was a downside, though. I had to wear a uniform. It wasn't the jeans or the white shirt that bothered me. It wasn't even the tacky khaki vest that I had to wear. It was the hat. It was an ugly hat. A professional clown would blush to wear this ridiculously ugly hat. It was brightly colored all the way around from top to bottom. A beaded wire stuck straight up from the center of the hat and, to add insult to injury, on top of that wire was a brightly colored propeller. This great American corporation had selected a propeller-topped hat as its signature image. If I wanted this job, I had to wear it. So there I was, six feet seven inches tall, college-educated, and my world had come down to this. I looked like an oversized clown who had escaped from a circus. My family laughed at me every time they saw me wearing that joke on my head.

The job and the hat did pay the bills, however, and more. I was finally able to give my children more than just the necessities. I was able to buy a new car for us, and the kids got the latest video game system for Christmas, as well as new clothes when they needed them and trips to amusement parks that had been out of our reach until then. We enjoyed our new sense of financial independence. However, along with the money came the selling of my soul and the pledging of my allegiance to "the hat."

The studio opened right on schedule. The grand opening was a spectacular event with balloon-making clowns and oversized dancing bears. The actual opening day was the largest in the company's history, breaking all records and making me an instant superstar in the eyes of the company.

With my newfound status came more responsibility. The company decided it would be great if I choreographed new store openings across the country. From Las Vegas to Buffalo, I spread the wealth and joy that went along with allegiance to "the hat." Sometimes I was gone two weeks at a time. With each new opening, a new company record was broken and my status continued to rise. All through that year my praises were sung from one state to the next. By January 2001 I was elected president of the mall merchants' board, which added even more duties to my already busy schedule. To top it all off, not only was I traveling throughout the country spreading my wisdom, I was also training every new manager the company hired.

Back home, although the money kept flowing in, I had missed band concerts, teacher conferences, and weekend baseball games. My kids saw less and less of me, and they didn't like it. I promised to spend more time with them, but each time I did a new disaster took me away. I was living out of a suitcase. My clothes were unpacked long enough for them to be washed, dried, and repacked before I hopped on another plane that would whisk me away to another grand opening or to clean up some mess that another over-tired trainer had left behind.

5

Three-bedroom house for rent in Union. Full in-town living. Near most schools and the city park. Perfect for families. A full country kitchen with up-to-date amenities. Large living and dining area with original woodwork intact. Two bathrooms with mudroom. Full basement with fruit cellar attached. Large front porch and backyard perfect for children. The right house at the right price for the right family. If interested, please contact . . .

* * *

The phone call came the following evening just after we had finished dinner. "It's a lovely home, just full of historic charm," said the man. "Do you have a lot of furniture? This house can hold a large amount of furniture."

Listening to him, I was sure that the house would be outside of my price range. "The rental price is $600 a month."

Great, I groaned to myself. The house sounded great, and it was large enough, so for six hundred bucks it had to be a shack.

"We will be holding an open house on Sunday if you would care to come," he said.

The words *open house* sent my heart into my stomach, but I took down the address anyway.

"Be there at one o'clock sharp," he said as he hung up.

Knowing others would be viewing the house on Sunday, I made a mental note to arrive twenty minutes early to be sure I would be the first one to fill out an application.

Sunday finally rolled around, and, as in the past, the boys stayed with my parents. After we got them settled, Lydia and I left for the open house; we were on a mission. If what the man on the telephone had said was true, we were going to do anything we had to do to rent this house. To my pleasure, as we pulled up in front of the house a good twenty-five minutes early, we were the first ones there.

Stepping out of the car, we looked the house over. Two large oak trees spread and shaded the front of the two-story house. The house was white with a large front porch. Two upstairs windows peeked out of the foliage, jutting out onto the roof as dormers. The windows were like peeking eyes observing the world. The house looked freshly painted and well taken care of; however, the yard had been ignored and needed a good raking. Leaves from the trees above had obviously been ignored. The boxed-in areas on the sides of the porch had probably contained flowers once upon a time, but now they were empty and needed to be cleaned. A set of concrete steps led up to a walkway that ended at the wooden stairs of the porch. Large, white paint containers sat waiting for someone to use the contents to freshen up the weary porch.

Nothing a good coat of paint can't fix, I thought to myself as I knocked on the door.

It was opened immediately by a man wearing overalls. "You must be here for the open house?"

At our nods, he said, "Well, Mr. Winters isn't here yet. He always runs a little late, but you're welcome to come on in and wait." With this, he stepped aside and motioned us into the house.

"I'm the maintenance man. I do little jobs here and there for Mr. Winters. Right now I'm working on some things that became weakened by the flood."

Alarmed, I asked, "This house wasn't in the flood, was it?"

"No, of course not," he assured me. "We did have some trees lose some limbs. Had to re-shingle the whole roof and we waited a year to begin rebuilding the breezeway on the back. We used to have a porch back there that collapsed when something gave way from the washing run-off water beneath it. Nothing to worry about though. We have all of that taken care of now."

I was sure this house had to be several blocks from the worst part of the flood, but his response put my mind at ease.

"Let me show you around a little while we wait for Mr. Winters to get here."

To Lydia's and my surprise, we found ourselves standing in a living room with a cherub border adorning the tops of the walls. The original woodwork was intact and large wooden columns ran to the ceiling, creating a divider that we would later realize separated the living room from the family room. The house had two floors, three bedrooms, and a large family kitchen with a mudroom that led to the back door. The upstairs bedrooms connected to a breezeway that could be accessed from either room. There was a bathroom at the bottom of the stairs and another in the mudroom.

Coming back downstairs, the man escorted us into the kitchen where we met an elderly man, in his seventies perhaps, entering the kitchen from the family room. "I am so sorry I'm late, but I see Ben has been showing you around."

This man was one of the strangest people I have ever seen. The moment I saw him, I knew he was eccentric. From beneath a cockeyed wig, his wrinkled face was a pale white; the only thing that brightened it were his red lips. His clothing only added to his clownish appearance. Apparently, he had a penchant for bright woolen shirts and sweaters even in warm weather. The image he presented to us was dizzying. Extending his right hand to firmly shake mine, he used his other hand to push back his wig, which had slipped over his forehead and threatened to cover his face.

"I am Mr. Winters. You may call me Carl. I am the owner of this property," he announced in a raspy voice, grabbing a clipboard from the counter next to him. "This is a beautiful kitchen, isn't it? They don't make kitchens like this anymore. Large like this and all," he said, grandly waving his claw-like hands.

"Notice how the windows are so nicely located over the sink. And the refrigerator; the refrigerator dispenses not only *ice*, but *ice water*, too!" Apparently this was the big lure Mr. Winters relied on to reel in new tenants. "And," he concluded triumphantly, "who could live without the convenience of a dishwasher?" He had obviously never debated that point with my mother.

Mr. Winters showed us the house as if we were on a museum tour, not potential renters. "Now," he said, "this house was built in the 1930s. The mudroom attached to the kitchen was there for the menfolk who came home from work all dirty. They could clean up there before entering the houses that their wives had spent all day cleaning."

Turning to me, he asked, "Do you have a wife, Mr. LaChance?"

I knew he would ask that question sooner or later; he had chosen sooner. I briefly explained that I was divorced and a parent. Upon hearing that, Mr. Winters turned to Lydia and asked, "Well, then, my little angel, you must be the lady of the house. How do you like the large, beautiful kitchen?"

Twelve-year-old Lydia, not pleased at all, managed to mumble something that sounded like "fine." And with that, Mr. Winters directed us to the basement.

"I am in the process of replacing this wallpaper," he said. The wallpaper he indicated lined the walls heading down to the basement. It was neon bright with large flowers. Where it had peeled away, it left large, bare patches.

To Lydia and me, the basement was a basement. To Mr. Winters it was a masterpiece of great historical significance. "See here," he said, pointing to the ceiling, "that's a butcher shower the men used to clean themselves after they had slaughtered the hogs. Obviously, they couldn't use the mudroom for that dirty job."

Pushing his wig back into place, he opened a door. "This is the fruit cellar. In the old days this is where the ladies of the house would keep their canned goods and cured meats for the long winter ahead."

The fruit cellar turned out to be a small room with a concrete ledge that acted as a shelf. There were steps that led up to slanted double doors, which in turn led out to the side yard.

This was more house than we ever imagined getting for the price, and Lydia and I were determined we were going to get it. Anyone who has ever lived in an apartment with three children will understand our desperation. We had to have this house. Our tour concluded with Mr. Winters handing us an application. I hurriedly filled it out and attached a check for the application fee. By this time, there were many other people looking at the house so we knew we would have to compete to be its tenants.

I handed the application to Mr. Winters. "Here you are, Mr. Winters. I am sure you'll find everything in order."

He smiled. His wig had slipped almost to the point of covering his eyebrows. "Call me Carl. Now, you *do* understand the responsibility that comes with living in an old house such as this?"

"Oh, yes. I understand. It's beautiful," I responded quickly, although I wasn't completely sure just what it was I was agreeing to.

"Well, then," he said brightly, "I will get back to you." With that parting comment, he was off to begin his next historical tour with more of the eager house hunters.

"What do you think?" I asked Lydia as we drove off.

"The house is perfect, and I hope we get it. That man is another story, though. He is so strange," Lydia said with a giggle. What could I do but agree with her? And we both began to laugh.

6

We've all heard the saying that hindsight is 20/20, and I guess that maxim applies in this situation as well. Who knows how quickly evil can attach itself to a family, how quickly it can make the decision to take that family down the darkest of pathways? When things began happening, I thought nothing of it. I always found an excuse. Looking back now, I think I'd be naive to believe that evil had set its sights on my family from the moment I walked into the old white house. A chain of events had already been set into motion long before that, events I had unknowingly helped set into motion. A chain of events that would change my life.

* * *

The night following our first visit to the old white house, I woke up to the sound of ten-year-old Matthew screaming. Sitting up, I listened. It was uncommon for him to have a bad dream and not wake up, especially after he'd made such a commotion. I sat in the darkness and listened, quiet.

Then I heard the running of feet, and Matthew's scared voice calling, "Daddy? Daddy?" My bedroom door flew open and the light flashed on. "Daddy, he was in my room. He was in my room!" Matthew was wide-eyed and very much awake. "He was in my room," he repeated.

In my best calm, daddy voice, I asked Matthew who was in his room. He looked into my eyes. He was obviously scared because I could feel him shaking through the bed covers.

"A man," he said.

I shifted into my "no monster here" routine and walked Matthew by the hand back to his room. "C'mon, let's go check it out."

I turned on the bedroom lights, and Michael's head popped out from underneath his covers on the top bunk. "What's going on?" he asked in a sleep-slurred voice.

"Go back to sleep, Michael. Matthew's just had a bad dream." With this, Michael was back under his covers and asleep in an instant.

Matthew and I looked around the room. "See? No man here."

Matthew pointed toward the corner. "He was over there, Daddy. I saw him. He was standing right there."

I went over and stood in the place Matthew indicated. "He's not here now." Our search went into high gear and I looked under the bed, in the closet, behind the bedroom door, in the bathroom, and in the shower. As we checked each area I made the same comment, "No man here."

Once we had searched the entire apartment, including the balcony (in case this was a smart man and he had decided to hide there), I took Matthew into my bedroom and tucked him into my bed.

"He was there, Daddy. Really. I saw him," Matthew's scared little voice said from beneath the covers.

"I believe you saw something, but remember, sometimes your mind can play tricks on you."

Matthew persisted. "This was no trick. He was there."

With this, I tucked him in bed tighter and told him I would be right back.

"Leave the lights on, Daddy."

I went down the hall into the kitchen for a drink of water. It was always so dry in the apartment when the air conditioner was on. As usual, the water felt better than it tasted. Rinsing my cup, I headed back down the long hall to my bedroom. "Okay, ready? Lights out."

I was looking down the hall as I turned out the light, and I saw the shadow of a man run by. I turned the light back on. Nothing there. I laughed as I turned out the light and headed for bed. *The little guy has really gotten to me*, I thought. Now *I* was seeing things.

"What's so funny?" Matthew asked.

"You are, Smelly. You are." With this, Matthew gave me a big kick, a kick I deserved since I wasn't supposed to use that name anymore.

"Good night, Matthew."

"Good night, old man." Matthew muffled his giggles as he snuggled closer to my back.

Later that night it was my turn to have a nightmare. It was one of those nightmares in which you think you're awake, but you're not. Those are the worst, not being able to tell the difference. It was surreal, the kind of nightmare that catches its victims by surprise. At the time (if I was awake, but I wasn't; this was a dream, right?) I could swear that it was really happening to me, but it wasn't.

"Look at me." The raspy voice came from somewhere in my dark bedroom.

"Look at me." The voice was more insistent this time.

"*See me.*" The room was dark, darker than the darkest of nights.

I raised myself up on my elbow and said, "Who's there?" No answer. I asked again, "Who's there?" When there was no response, I convinced myself that I was hearing things and closed my eyes, lying down to go back to sleep. Instantly I felt a pressure on my chest. It felt like someone was leaning on me, pushing me down into the bed, *pinning* me to it. I couldn't move, and it was so dark I couldn't see anything.

"You know you want to look at me." The voice whispered into my ear. Each word was punctuated by a foul stench. I couldn't move, I couldn't fight, I couldn't scream.

"Look at me, for I am *glorious!*"

"Please, God," I managed to whisper from beneath the weight of the thing on top of me.

"God isn't here. God doesn't exist. You've said so yourself, haven't you?" Now the pressure became tremendous. *"Look at me,"* the voice commanded.

I could see it; the white of its eyes glowed in the dark. I began to struggle, but I couldn't get away. With each effort to free myself, I was crushed deeper into the bed. I saw its white ghostly hands right before I felt them wrap around my neck.

"God isn't here. It's just . . . " It paused and revealed its face to me: the face of Christ possessed, Christ gone mad. " . . . *me.*"

With this I woke up with a start, sitting straight up in bed.

"No!" My words rang in my head. My heart pounded. "Just a nightmare, just a nightmare," I repeated over and over. "Just a nightmare." I would sleep no more that night.

7

The next morning began like any other Monday morning. Everyone had to get cleaned, dressed, and fed before leaving the house. The crackle of my cereal woke me up as I poured milk into the bowl. It had been a bad night. I hadn't had a nightmare like that since my early twenties, and I was still trying to shake off its spell.

Lydia and Michael were fighting over the bathroom. Normally I would have broken it up as soon as they uttered their first hateful words, but that morning was different. No matter what they said to each other or to me, they got no response from me. I was finally brought out of my hypnotic state by the slamming of my daughter's bedroom door. My dream had been too intense, and the last thing I needed was daytime drama. Finally, everyone was dressed, backpacks in hand, and we headed for the door. There were only a few more weeks of school left, and for that I was thankful.

The week itself passed without much fanfare, but each day brought us no news about the house either, so our anxiety increased proportionately. Where would we go if we didn't get this house? There hadn't been any suitable listings in either of the papers that week. We had to get it.

The phone call came Sunday night, a week later, at eight o'clock.

"Mr. LaChance? This is Carl Winters. I have selected you out of the many candidates who looked at the house. You are still interested, aren't you?"

Interested? Of course I was! I was biting at the bit.

"Well, then, you have yourself a beautiful new home."

We agreed to meet the following day at a restaurant not far from my work, where I would sign the lease and give him the first and last month's rent for the house. I thought this arrangement was a bit odd, and I was disappointed because I couldn't wait to see the house again.

"Wouldn't it be easier, Mr. Winters, to meet you at the house about seven tonight?"

"Oh, no," he said immediately. "Oh, no, *simply* impossible. I have a great many errands to run, and they're to finish painting the front porch today. I'm afraid we would simply be in the way." I recognize defeat when I'm faced with it, and I knew better than to argue with him. We would meet at the restaurant the next day.

I arrived fifteen minutes early the next day and waited in the car with the air conditioning running in an attempt to stave off the day's heat and humidity. Our meeting time came and went. Fifteen minutes passed and he hadn't appeared. Thirty minutes, forty-five minutes, and he still wasn't there. I called the number that had been in the ad, but his answering machine picked up. All I could do was leave a message. I was angry and about to give up and leave when I saw him pull into the parking lot.

I greeted him at his car, where he frantically arranged his wig with one hand as he gathered papers off the front seat and stuffed them into a briefcase with the other.

"I am *so* sorry I'm late. I let the time get away from me and then the traffic was just horrible."

We went into the restaurant and sat down. To my surprise he ordered a hamburger, and I had to force myself to sit calmly and watch him eat. At one point mustard dripped from the burger, down his chin, and all over his wool jacket, which was totally unsuitable for a hot Missouri day.

"I'm so messy," he exclaimed, making an attempt to clean himself up. Then he excused himself and went to the men's room.

Meanwhile, I sat and fumed.

When he returned, he pulled all the papers from his briefcase and we proceeded to go through the lease point by point as he read every word to me. Finally I was able to sign the lease, and I gave him a check, expecting to receive the keys to the house in return.

"Now," he announced, "I will meet you at the house on Thursday afternoon at about two o'clock for a walk-through. I want to be very thorough, so we'll need a few hours to get through it."

There was no way I could meet Mr. Winters on Thursday at two in the afternoon. I had to work. The earliest I could possibly meet him would be six. He became noticeable fidgety with my counterproposal.

"Well, I suppose that will have to do. I must leave there before dark, though. I do hate driving at night."

I explained again why we would have to meet in the evening, and he reluctantly agreed. We would do our walk-through on Thursday evening, and I would be able to start moving in on Friday. I left him sitting at the table, using my children as an excuse to leave him. As I got into my car, I wondered what more he could possibly show me in a two hour walk-through after last Sunday's "museum" tour. I began to worry just a tiny bit. After all, I had just given that man all of my savings so I could move into his house. He had my check, and I still didn't have any keys. I could only hope that I was making the right decision to move into that house. It was too late to back out, however. And besides, I didn't have any other housing options. It was Mr. Winters' home or . . . well, or nothing.

8

Thursday night found me sitting in my car in front of the Union house. Despite the air conditioning, I was baking. We had agreed on six o'clock. It was already a quarter past that, and the old man was nowhere in sight. My head dropped to the steering wheel as the heat pushed me closer to despair. What was going on? I'd rushed out of work and broken at least seven laws (those were the ones I could count, anyway), and he was late. Of *course* he was late. He had been late to every appointment we'd made. Six-twenty. He still hadn't arrived.

I got out of the car to try to catch a breeze. I sat down on the ledge of the porch and immediately realized that my jeans were sticking to it. Wet paint. With the humidity, the paint still hadn't dried, and now I had a few paint spots on the back of my pants. I couldn't sit on the porch so I sat on the concrete steps that led up to it. As I sat waiting for Mr. Winters, I absentmindedly observed a trail of ants work their way up the steps, over the tops of my shoes, and up my leg. The heat must have lulled me into a trance, for with the first ant bite I realized what I had been watching and started patting myself down. I was still killing ants when Mr. Winters finally pulled up at 6:31.

I was deliberating the wisdom of going from slapping ants to slapping a ridiculously tardy old man when I heard his voice. "Have you been waiting long?" he asked with a wave.

"Just a little while," I replied through my clenched jaw. My mother had trained me well, but I couldn't help thinking that the feel of my palm smacking his wrinkled old cheeks would feel mighty good.

His wig bounced up and down as he walked up the stairs to where I was standing.

"Traffic was just horrible," he said, forgetting that I had driven through the same streets, but I bit my lip.

"Shall we get started?" His voice trailed away from me as he began walking to the side of the house. "Let's go in the back door because I don't think the porch paint has had time to dry."

Oh, how I wished looks could kill as I followed behind him.

It was nice and cool in the house. "New insulation," Mr. Winters said. "Now, let's begin in the living room." Taking a pen from his winter wool jacket, he straightened his wig again. In the living room he opened the blinds to let in the light. "We need to be able to see!" he remarked. We covered every possible inch of the downstairs. We looked at everything, right down to the slats on each blind and the functioning of each window. Upon completing our downstairs inspections, we headed for the stairs to go to the second floor.

"You don't believe in ghosts, do you, Mr. LaChance?" he asked casually.

"No, I don't," I replied. "Why do you ask?"

"Well, I haven't heard any such nonsense about *this* house having ghosts; however, not everyone can live in an old house such as this."

With this, he hastened me up the steps. "We had better hurry. Not too much daylight left."

The upstairs inspection went much faster than the downstairs inspection had, and we were through very quickly. We had just finished up when the icemaker in the kitchen refrigerator completed its cycle and dropped a load of ice into its container with a bang. The old man nearly jumped clear out of his wig.

"What was that?" he asked, trying to catch his breath.

"It was the refrigerator icemaker," I replied, puzzled.

He sighed with relief.

"Mr. Winters, that's not a great way to make your new tenant feel comfortable with the house," I joked with him, laughing. He finally laughed too, and was still laughing as he handed me the keys and headed for the back door.

"I do wish I could stay and chat longer, but I must get home. I will call you this weekend," and with that he was gone.

I stood for a moment, admiring the house. *A real house with a real yard*, I thought as I walked to my car. This was everything and more that we had ever imagined for ourselves. It wasn't going to be just a house, either; the kids and I were going to make it our home. As I drove away, I didn't notice that the lights in the house were coming on, one by one.

9

The stress I had suppressed over the six years since my wife aban-doned us crashed down on me the night before we moved to the Union house. I had spent those years healing my children, but I had forgotten to heal myself. But isn't that what a dad did? Pick up the pieces and try to live as normally as possible for the sake of the children? I had never made time to deal with what *I* had lost, and each time I'd felt myself losing my grip, I pushed those feelings from my mind. I didn't have time for sissy emotions. I was a man with respon-sibilities.

Other than my children, I was alone. I had met my wife when I was twelve years old, and she had been one of my closest friends for all those years. When she left, I didn't just lose a wife; I lost a best friend. We had been social as a couple, but I had no close friends to speak of, the natural progression of being married with kids. Besides, I was already living with my best friend. Who else did I need? My kids were getting older and forming their own circles of friends. Here I was, a man who had been attached to one woman for all of his life and I was out in a world where I didn't know how to relate to other people, especially women. What could I talk about? How to get dirty socks white again? How to cook dinners on Sunday and then use that wonderful Seal-o-Matic to keep them fresh for a hot meal for the kids on a busy day? I would find myself in social situations without the ability to carry on an adult conversation with strangers. As a result, I put everything that was me into my kids.

In retrospect, I realize that I was going through a deep depression, but at the time it was just my life. I never allowed myself to dwell on any one thought about myself or my past life; I just kept pushing those thoughts away, tucking them into the back recesses of my mind for another day, another time when I might have time to deal with them. For now, however, I didn't have time to indulge a cold, much less own up to the fact that I might need therapy. I had to keep it together for the sake of my children.

It had become so bad for Lydia at home that she had actually been happy to see her mother leave. And Matthew, the child that his mother had always resented, went looking for mother figures everywhere, especially at school. He would become so attached to his female teachers that for him the last day of school was like losing his mother again and again.

Michael, however, was the child I really had to worry over and concentrate on. The day his mother left, he ran to her and held on to her legs. "Mommy, please don't go," he begged. She pulled his arms away from her and threw him to the ground. He began to scream. The scream of a broken heart. Had it not been my worry for him that day, I would have killed her, I am sure of that. I picked him up and held him as he continued cry, wail, scream. Michael did nothing but cry for a solid year after my wife left, so I couldn't let go. You can understand, then, why I had never allowed myself to mourn the death of my marriage. There was no time for me to grieve. I had to keep myself going for the sake of my children. The dam that held all my emotions in check broke, though, the night before the move. All my pain and all my fears came rushing out in a dream.

I was totally exhausted when I went to bed that night. It was nearly midnight, and packing up our belongings and the stress I had gone through trying to find a new place for us to move were taking their toll on me. After I sealed the last box, I checked on each of the kids, a habit I'd formed when they were infants. Everyone was safely in bed asleep, and it was finally my turn. I was asleep as soon as I hit the bed; I began dreaming almost immediately.

The kids and I were living in our new house. Everything was unpacked and put away. It was almost like an episode of Leave It to Beaver, *minus June Cleaver. The bright sun shone through the windows; everything looked so white, fresh, and clean. There was a knock at the door, more of a pounding actually, and I went to see who was there. It was probably one of our new neighbors stopping by to welcome us to the block. Instead, my ex-wife was on the porch holding something in her hands.*

As soon as I noticed that, the dream's mood changed. Storm clouds began raging through the sky. Lightning was crackling and thunder crashing. She shoved her bundle into my arms.

"I told you before, I can't be a mother." Her voice echoed throughout the house. Then she turned and ran away. I must have been in shock, because she was gone and the door was closed before I understood the impact of what had just happened. Then the bundle in my arms moved. Pulling back the cover, I discovered I was holding a baby, a baby with crystal-blue eyes in a shade I had never seen before.

Then Lydia came to me and asked, "What is that?"
I looked at her in shock and said, "It's a baby. It's our baby."
With that, I began to cry.

When I woke from the dream, I was clutching my pillow and weeping. The floodgates had opened, and it wasn't going to be easy to shut them again. I've heard people refer to the hours between midnight and six a.m. as the lonely hours, the suicide hours. That night I fully understood what they mean.

The baby in that dream still haunts me. Did it represent a child my wife and I were supposed to have? What if she had left me before we had claimed all of the souls that God had intended for us? Had her leaving created an awful wrinkle in God's plans for us?

10

The morning after my dream was moving day. We rented one of those trucks with the dinosaur painted boldly on the side. Eleven-year-old Michael was thrilled at the idea of a dinosaur moving van and filled me in on all of its characteristics so I would know exactly what sort of creature we were dealing with. He offered much too much information for me to comprehend at eight in the morning.

The day was horribly hot and humid, and as we lugged boxes and furniture down the stairs, I gave the kids strict instructions to pop me in the head if I ever again had the bright idea to rent an apartment above the first floor. It wasn't long before I was tired, exhausted, and cranky. My mood wasn't helped when the couch with its heavy oak base got stuck on the stairway. As hard as we tried, we couldn't budge it. It was another thirty minutes before we finally got the couch freed and onto the truck. Three hours later we shut the doors on the jumbo dinosaur truck.

My dad had come over to drive the truck; I was to follow him in the car. As he maneuvered the truck out of the parking lot, I stood near the back of it to make sure he didn't hit anything. We were safely on the street when an upstairs neighbor came out to cap off my day.

"Hey!" he yelled at us. "You hit my car!"

I had been standing right there, and I knew that Dad hadn't come close to his car.

"See! Look right here where you hit my car."

Sure enough there was a dent down low on the driver's side of the car. In fact, the dent was so low that the truck couldn't have possibly caused it. This guy was trying to take us on an insurance-scam joyride, and by now I'd had enough of this dysfunctional neighborhood.

"He didn't come close to hitting your car," I said.

"I didn't hit your car," my father stated calmly but firmly.

"Yes, you did, you asshole!"

Dad either noticed that my face had turned beet red or he saw that my hands were clenched into fists, and he continued to try to defuse the situation.

"Young man, I didn't hit your car," he repeated calmly but firmly.

"Yes, you did, asshole. You hit my fucking car." My dad walks with a cane due to an accident he had years before. At this point, Dad tightened his grip on his cane.

"There is no need for you to use that language in front of my granddaughter." With this, my dad threw his cane to the ground; he was ready to fight.

Sensing that if this went much further the guy was going to be picking himself up off the pavement, I said, "If I were you, I would shut up now and walk away. We didn't hit your car. We didn't come near your car. And if you don't watch your language, I'm going to have to wipe this street up with your ass. Now go!"

With this the guy left, yelling that he was calling the police, who shortly thereafter arrived on the scene. They looked at the truck and listened to both sides of the story.

"Is the truck insured?" asked one of the officers.

Of course it was; I had taken the insurance along with the rental. And that was all it took. I gave the guy the information he needed about the truck, the police officers left, and Dad, the kids, and I drove off, too, glad to finally be out of that awful neighborhood. It irritated me that the guy with the banged-up truck got his car fixed for free. I just knew that he had spent the entire morning figuring out a scheme. It paid off, and Christmas came early for him.

As we pulled away, our downstairs neighbor came out of his apartment and flipped me the bird. I slowly pulled the car away as I yelled out the window at him, "Fuck you, fat boy."

Thank God my dad was on his way down the street with his granddaughter sitting next to him in the front seat.

We pulled up in front of our new house shortly after two in the afternoon. We got the front door open, set up the truck ramps, and began unloading. I was removing the last few items when a car slowed down, almost stopping in front of our new home. "Hope you get along okay here," called the passenger, and then the car sped up and drove away.

"What do you think of that, Dad?" my daughter asked, slightly puzzled.

"Friendly neighbors, I suppose," I replied as I shut the sliding door to the truck.

11

Our first night in the house passed with little fanfare. Maybe it was because we were so tired. Who knows if there was a rhyme or a reason for what was about to begin.

We camped out in the living room that night. By the time everyone had been fed and cleaned, I was too exhausted to even think about putting beds together. That task would have to wait until the next day. The kids had taken care of their own priorities; they had set up the television and the PlayStation. As I drifted off to sleep, they tried to find some fantasy treasure.

The next morning we were up and began unpacking boxes and settling into our new home. As we moved about the house, this time unencumbered by Mr. Winters, I noticed something odd. Each of the interior doors had an old-fashioned hook and eye latch, but they weren't located on the inside of the doors, so anyone within the room could maintain privacy—but on the *outside* as if to keep someone *in* the room.

"Why is that, Dad?" asked Matthew.

"Beats me," I replied, and continued unpacking our things.

I started with the main living areas. I figured the kids could each take care of their own rooms until I was ready to set up their beds. The kitchen was the obvious place to begin. I had bought myself some time by buying donuts the day before, but I knew the kids would be gnawing my ankles if I wasn't prepared to fix them something for lunch.

First, the kitchen had to be cleaned, and I wanted to make sure that it was clean to my standards. I was ahead in the cleaning game because I had already done the bathrooms the night before.

I could hear the boys running across the upstairs floors and it sounded like they were having fun playing. Lydia was with me, helping place our dishes into the cabinets. This was a big deal for her, and she had already mapped out in her mind where everything should go. Between us, the kitchen was done in no time at all. We had just finished the kitchen when Matthew arrived, on schedule, asking about lunch. It seemed a shame to mess up our newly cleaned and organized kitchen, so it was fast-food hamburgers for lunch, which suited me just fine and made the kids happy. After lunch, we went back home to start on the living room and family room.

Lydia decided that a large picture of two angels should be hung in the living room, where it would complement the cherub wall-paper border that surrounded the room. I hammered a nail in the wall, straightened the picture a bit, and turned to walk away. *Crash*. I turned back to see that the picture had fallen to the floor. I picked it up and examined it. The frame and the hanger on the back seemed okay, so I re-hung the picture. I turned away and *crash*. The picture was on the floor again. Slightly irritated, I hung it a third time, but this time, when I turned and began to walk away, I felt a rush of air and something hit the back of my ankles. "What the hell . . ." I turned to see the picture lying at my feet. More determined than ever, I hung the picture a fourth time, this time adding, "Stay there, dammit." Perhaps a bit of profanity would be all the glue the picture needed to stay on the wall. Besides, there wasn't anyone there to hear me; the kids were playing on the front porch.

"Dad, come and see this," my daughter's voice rang through the front door. I stepped out onto the porch. I had been unpacking for hours and I needed a break. "Sit down and watch this," she said excitedly.

"Watch what?" No sooner were the words out of my mouth when my daughter pointed to an old man walking down the sidewalk toward our house. When he reached our property line, he quickly crossed the street and continued his walk on the opposite sidewalk.

"People don't like walking in front of our house, Dad. Isn't that weird?" my daughter whispered, still breathless with excitement.

And right she was. We sat on our porch for a good long time, watching as our neighbors crossed the street to avoid walking directly in front of our house. After a while we began to make it a game. Someone would come right to the property line, and then off they went across the street. Lydia's infectious giggle caused me to laugh every time it happened. A couple of times I waved to them as if to say hello, but they just dropped their heads and continued on, hastening their pace. Lydia would break into delighted laughter.

"Maybe they're uncomfortable with new neighbors," I rationalized, trying to make sense out of the senseless, and we went inside for dinner.

I couldn't help but notice that the house was really cold. Apparently the air conditioner was in great condition; it didn't seem to have any trouble keeping the house comfortable. *A little* too *comfortable*, I thought as I turned up the thermostat a couple of degrees.

Dinner that night was frozen pizza, and afterward Lydia and I went upstairs to set up her bed; she just had to sleep in her new room. The boys stayed downstairs watching one of their many favorite movies. In no time at all, Lydia's bed was together and we went downstairs to do the same with my bed. My bed, with its wrought-iron canopy, was more of a chore than either of us had bargained for. After a few hours, though, it was ready to accommodate me and the two sleeping boys out in the living room. I wasn't setting up their beds, as I had already decided to buy them new ones the following weekend. Both boys were getting too big for their twin bunk beds, and I had to tuck their limbs safely into place every night.

Somewhere between midnight and eight in the morning, Lydia found her way downstairs. I found her in bed with me and the boys when the alarm went off. "Lydia? What are you doing down here? I thought you were sleeping in your new room."

She looked at me with sleepy eyes and said, "I was, Daddy, but my closet door kept opening up. And it sounded like boxes were moving around in the other room. I got a little scared so I came down here."

I remember thinking, *Great, one more thing for my 'to do' list. Fixing the closet door.* I made a mental note of it and got the kids up so they could get ready for church.

12

Every Sunday morning we would go through the same routine, all of us rushing around trying to get ready, because my parents picked up the kids at precisely 8:30 so they could make it to Sunday school on time. Did I go to church? No. Between my marriage breaking up and Janice's death, I was completely turned off to the whole idea of organized religion. I had long ago lost my faith in anything that I couldn't see. How could I possibly know that my negative attitude toward faith was a clear invitation to the dance? Remember what Jack Nicholson said when he played the Joker in *Batman*: "Would you dance with the devil in the pale moonlight?" I would find the answer to that soon. Very soon. Without me knowing it or wanting it, the dance had already begun.

"Daddy, how do I look in this dress?" Lydia stood before me in a new pink sundress that her grandmother had recently bought for her.

"You look like a beautiful princess," I responded with a grin. With a turn of her skirt and a smile on her face, she went off to rule the rest of her castle. I heard her from the other room. "Matthew, you can't possibly think that looks good." She was right. Matthew came into my room wrinkled from head to toe, his shoes untied, almost tripping over his laces as he walked. "Come on, buddy, let's see if we can find something else for you to wear," I said.

Finally, after getting Matthew dressed, praising my daughter's beauty several more times, and begging Michael to hurry up, the kids were safely out the door and driving away in the back seat of my parents' car. I sat down on the couch with a huge sigh of relief. *Crash.* It sounded like a few of the boxes upstairs had fallen over. Obviously, Michael had been rummaging through things, and that was why it had taken him so long to get ready for church. It sounded to me like a mess he was going to have to clean up when he got home.

I dozed on the couch until I heard their excited footsteps on the porch. Matthew ran in, proclaiming proudly, "See the Joseph's Ark I made in Sunday school?" I looked at him with disbelief. I could never understand how he could spend every Sunday at church and still confuse the simplest of Bible stories.

"Matthew, that's Noah, not Joseph. Joseph was Jesus's dad."

A look of shock spread over Matthew's face. "Don't be silly, Dad. Jesus's dad was Moses."

I wasn't in the mood to get into a Scripture war with him, so I quickly changed the subject. "Let's get ready to do some work in the yard."

Filled with excitement, the children ran to their rooms to change into play clothes.

It probably seems odd that three kids would be excited about yard work. For the last several years, though, the only thing we had that resembled a yard was an eight-foot balcony overlooking a street and a parking lot. It wasn't only the kids who were excited to work in the yard; I was just as excited as they were.

It was a beautiful, sunny Sunday afternoon in late May. The humidity had finally cleared, leaving behind it perfect weather. We began by raking all the old leaves into piles. It seemed strange to be raking leaves in May, but I was glad to do it and I was enjoying the day. Next we mowed the grass. This, too, was a big deal for the kids as they took turns behind the mower. Once the grass had been cut, Lydia and I began trimming along the steps and the sidewalk that led around the side of the house.

"Dad," said Matthew, "we should clean up the sidewalk and water the grass."

He was right. There was a ton of grass clippings everywhere, and parts of the lawn were looking brown and in need of a good dowsing of water.

"Okay, you and Michael go down to the basement and get the garden hose and bring it out." Both boys ran off into the house laughing and giggling. A few minutes later Michael came out of the house alone.

"Where's Matthew?"

Michael shrugged his shoulders and said, "He should be right behind me."

Suddenly we heard screams from the house. In an instant I knew it was Matthew and there was something seriously wrong. I ran into the house through the front door, the living room, the family room, and into the kitchen. There was Matthew standing in the middle of the kitchen, shaking and pointing. Pointing at what? I tried to find what he wanted me to see as Lydia and Michael ran into the room.

"What's he pointing at?" they asked.

"Monster," whispered a frightened Matthew. Lydia and Michael began to giggle. Matthew was pointing at the basement door.

"A monster in the basement," he said quietly, without fully catching his breath.

Both of the other children broke out in full laughter, and I scolded them before sending them back outside. I turned to open the basement door, beginning the routine I had performed so many nights before in his bedroom at the apartment. He began to scream as my hand turned the doorknob.

"No, Dad, there's a monster in the basement. I know, it chased me up the stairs."

I opened the basement door and peeked around the corner. "No monster there, buddy." Walking down the basement steps, past the peeling neon flowers on the wall, I continued my mantra. "No monster on the steps," I said loudly so he could hear me. At the bottom of the stairs I looked around. "No monsters down here, Matthew. Come take a look."

"I think I'll stay up here," he responded in a trembling voice.

Walking back up the basement steps, I got my "no monster" speech ready. There was nothing there; I had looked. There was nothing going on but the active imagination of a young boy. At least that's what I thought as I consoled him.

"It's just your imagination, Matthew. We're in a new house and you're just a little bit nervous. Don't worry. Okay?" The monster had just been a leftover remnant in his mind. That's what I thought at the time. The days to come would change my mind.

As he walked to the kitchen door, Matthew turned back to me, fear still lingering in his eyes. "No monster?"

"Nothing there. No monster," I assured him, and then he was off outside to play.

The rest of the day was like a fantastic dream. It was a beautiful day, and we laughed and played water hose tag and made complete messes of ourselves. We couldn't have foreseen that it was one of the best days we would have for a long time to come. Things were about to change, and in our ignorance we played on.

At sunset we went inside to clean up. I decided it was too late to cook, so we went to Taco Bell. *Thank God for fast food*, I thought as the boys ran to the car, Lydia walking sedately at my side.

We were gone for no more than an hour, and it was almost completely dark when we returned. As I pulled up in front of the house, every light in the house seemed to be on. I commented to the children that they were going to have to get jobs if they planned to make a habit of leaving all the lights on. We walked inside and the frigid air hit us immediately. I adjusted the air-conditioner thermostat for the second time.

The rest of the evening went by as usual. The kids played video games and watched television. Lydia and Michael fought over what to watch. Michael, a big fan of the St. Louis Cardinals, wanted to watch the baseball game. They finally agreed on a video they could watch together instead of regular television; other than the game, there wasn't much on TV that they hadn't already seen. Matthew sat on the couch and played his Game Boy.

I was in the family room folding clothes and getting ready to put them away when Matthew walked by me.

"Where are you going, buddy?" I asked.

"Have to use the bathroom."

"Okay. Make sure you turn out the light," I said, remembering the light situation from earlier. I continued folding the laundry when once again I heard my son screaming. I caught him in midair as he ran through the kitchen door.

"What is going on with you?" I asked him, noticing that he was trembling as I grabbed his arm.

"It came after me again," he panted, trying to catch his breath.

With this, Michael cracked a joke about the basement monster, but he quickly stopped when his eyes met the glare of an angry father.

"Come on, Matthew, there are no monsters in this house. You're just imagining it," I said soothingly. I finally calmed him down to a point where he could tell me what had happened to him.

"I left the bathroom door opened so I could hear what you guys were doing. I looked up the steps and that's when I saw it. It was so horrible. It came rushing down the steps at me."

"Shush," I said, calming him down before he became too emotional again. "What came down the steps after you?" Nothing could have prepared me for what he was to say next. It was years before I would talk about it again.

"A clown, a monster clown came after me."

With this, Michael and Lydia began to laugh. Stopping them with another glare, I began to walk Matthew through the whole "no monster here" routine again, trying to convince him that everything was okay. He was safe. We were all safe. Safety, however, is only in the eye of the beholder, and Matthew didn't believe me for a moment.

With Matthew finally calmed down, we all went to bed. The boys were still bunking with me, and I lay there listening to their even breathing and worried about Matthew. What was going on with him, I wondered? Was it the move? Was he beginning to have trouble dealing with the divorce? Was he missing his mother? My musings were interrupted by my daughter's sleepy voice mumbling something about her closet door not staying shut. What was going on? It was becoming clear to me that something was happening; I just wasn't sure what it was. The kids drifted off to sleep, and a short while later I did the same in mid-thought.

Sometime in the middle of the night, a noise woke me up. Sitting up in bed, I looked at the doorway that led into the living room. To my utter astonishment, an old man wearing a red flannel shirt stood there. He was motionless, expressionless, just staring, staring at me and my three sleeping children. I rubbed my eyes. When I opened them again the doorway was empty. I laughed at myself as I lay back down. The kids were going to be the death of me. Now they had *me* seeing things. I laughed again as I drifted back to sleep.

13

All too soon, morning came with its usual rush to get everyone ready for school and out the door on time. The kids had their backpacks, and I had my stupid propeller hat. We ran to the car with just fifteen minutes to spare before the bell rang. In the daylight there was nothing out of the ordinary in the house, nothing out of place.

Work was its usual fast-paced, overly friendly, stab-you-in-the-back environment, and I couldn't wait to leave for home. I had so much to do and very little free time to do it before I had to fly off to Indianapolis. I knew the kids, especially Matthew, wouldn't be happy. Ever since his mother had left, he didn't like being apart from me for very long. I will never rid myself of the guilt I felt when he was younger and I had to pry his little arms from around my legs, running to the door so I could go to work. Now, with all of this travel time, he hated it even more. They all hated it.

I picked the kids up from my mom's right at six as usual. They had already eaten dinner and she always had a plate waiting for me. It was easier for everyone that way. Besides, at least I was sure they would get one good meal, usually a great meal, at least once a day, and it was better than the TV dinners I served when things got hectic.

This was the last week of school before summer vacation. The boys were excited because Little League baseball had started, and Lydia was nervous because this would be her first year playing softball. They talked about it all the way home and made plans for the summer that lay ahead. This seemed like a good time to tell them about my upcoming business trip. There were audible groans from the boys in the back seat, and Lydia instantly began trying to persuade me that instead of "inconveniencing" their grandparents, they should stay home. She was quite mature and *perfectly* capable of caring for herself and her brothers while I was gone. I decided this would also be a good time to tell them that I was taking a long weekend and that I wouldn't be leaving until Tuesday, so it wouldn't actually be a whole week. There were cheers from the back seat and groans from my daughter as I explained to her that she would, indeed, be going to Grandma's house with her brothers.

As I turned the corner onto our street, I saw that we had again left on all the lights in the house. Apparently my speeches about the high cost of electricity were falling on deaf ears. We walked into the house and settled in for a quiet, uneventful evening. It would turn out to be one of the few we would experience for some time to come.

We enjoyed the quiet evening, and the rest of the week passed by slowly as the kids anticipated the end of the school year. Something odd was going on though. Every day, when we left the house for school and work, I would make sure that all of the lights were turned off. Every night we would come home to find the house blazing brightly with every light on. And also, as I had done every evening since we had moved to the Union house, I made a quick sweep of the house, making sure that we were alone. And, as usual, I was satisfied that no one else was in the house. We were absolutely alone.

Later that evening I walked into the living room and felt a shock run through my body. It was like an electrical shock, but different. It started deep inside my body and worked its way out. Every hair on my arms and neck stood on end. Suddenly I felt very warm. The shock passed through me and was gone in an instant, leaving me and the living room icy cold. I concluded to myself that the shock was caused by some sort of electrical problem in the house, and I would speak to my dad about it the next day.

The kids were playing and I let them stay up a little too late. In return, I got them up a little too early because I was going to check out the lighting situation. I put both boys in the car, and Lydia and I went through the house together to make sure every light was off. Once satisfied, we looked at each other with a sense of accomplishment and left the house.

That morning I dropped the kids off at my mom and dad's, an event that signified the start of their summer vacation. Both of my parents were sitting at the kitchen table drinking their coffee, a morning routine they rarely missed.

"How are things over at the house?" Dad asked, looking at me over the rim of his World's Greatest Grandpa cup. This seemed like a perfect moment to tell him about my electrical problem.

"Well, now that you bring it up, there's been something strange going on over there this week. When we come home at night, every light in the house is on."

My mother rinsed out her flowered mug at the sink; talking to me over her shoulder, she said, "The kids are probably leaving them on before you leave." She returned to sit at the table next to my father. I was leaning on the counter, which I quickly stopped doing when I noticed the glare that only a mother can muster when correcting her child.

"Maybe so. Yeah, you're probably right. But last night I felt like this electrical charge went through me when I was in the living room."

Dad gave me a puzzled look.

"I think we may have some electrical problems," I explained.

"I really don't see how that's possible," he said. "Your mom's absolutely right. You're probably leaving the lights on and not paying attention. It happens all the time here. As for that electrical feeling thing, I'll come over and check it out tomorrow morning."

Relieved, I looked at both my parents and said, "Thanks. I wish you would. And as for the lights, Lydia and I made sure they were off before we left today. We'll see what happens tonight." With that, it was time for me to go. I kissed the kids, and as I was walking out I heard them clamoring over what kind of cereal would be best that morning. The last thing I heard was "Cookie Crisp" as I headed to the car.

Finally, work was over for the week. I really needed the long weekend ahead of me. Of course, I wasn't looking forward to my trip the next week. Who would? It was Indiana, for God's sake. Not much different from where I was living. Why couldn't it be Las Vegas again? That was a great trip and a profitable one.

Anxious to get home, I picked up the kids and we headed straight there. As I turned the corner onto our street, I found myself holding my breath, and I began to laugh. It was Lydia's voice that brought me back to reality.

"Daddy, look! They're all on again."

A surge of panic ran through me as I pulled up to the house. Someone had to have been in the house since we left that morning. I ran from the car and through the front door. I checked the living room, the family room, the kitchen, my room, the boys' room upstairs, the bathroom, the basement. Nothing. There was no one there and nothing was out of place as far as I could tell.

I picked up the phone to call our landlord, Mr. Winters. After the usual courtesies, I got to the point.

"Mr. Winters, have you been inside this house anytime this week?"

He seemed a little indignant at my question, but I didn't care. "No, Mr. LaChance. I would give you twenty-four hours' notice before I came in or sent in a maintenance person to do a repair. Why do you ask?"

Trying to not anger him, I replied, "Well, the past couple of nights when I've come home, all of the lights have been on."

I could hear him clearing his throat. "Ah, I see. Perhaps the children left them on?" he suggested.

I assured him that wasn't the case, especially since Lydia and I had made such a point just that morning of checking each light before we left.

"Well, you know these old houses, Mr. LaChance. You can never tell. Would you feel better if I had someone come out and check it for you? It *could* be electrical, you know." I declined his offer, explaining that my father would be over the next day to check out the electrical box.

After I hung up the phone I stood there for a moment, thinking about that odd old man. The telephone rang, bringing me to my senses. It was my father calling to see if everything had been okay when we got home.

"No, things weren't okay," I told him. "The lights were on."

The next morning the kids were excited to see Grandpa pull up in front of the house. We went to the basement, and he took a good look at the electrical box and the wiring.

"Well, doesn't seem to be a problem here. Better have the landlord put a door on this circuit box though." He turned around, looking at the wall where a showerhead hung down. "That's a butcher shower, Steven." I asked him what he meant and he said, "That's where the farmers used to clean up after slaughtering, before going upstairs to their wives. Don't see many of those anymore."

Turning out the basement light, I looked back at the shower. "What the hell do I need one of them for?" I wondered.

We sat on the couch in the living room to talk. Dad was telling the kids they had better be ready the next morning when he came by to pick them up for church. Suddenly, something heavy fell on the floor upstairs, directly above our heads.

"What was that?" my dad asked, looking up.

"I don't know. Maybe a box fell over." As I said that, I looked over at my father and saw tears in his eyes. He was holding out his arm, staring at it.

"What in the hell is *this*!" He seemed a little disturbed.

"Um, that's that electrical feeling I was telling you about, Dad."

"That's no electrical feeling I've ever felt before," he said in a concerned voice. "I don't know what the hell that was." With that, he got up, mumbling something about needing to get his lawn mowed. He kissed the children, and as he headed for his truck I heard another box fall on the floor above me. "See you in the morning," he said.

Watching my father drive away, I contemplated the electrical problem. What could be causing the strange anomaly? The kids began playing in the yard. A normal Saturday lay ahead of us. A good Saturday.

14

It was a normal Sunday in every respect. I was taking a long weekend and enjoying it, for the most part. On Tuesday I would be on a
plane bound for Indianapolis and wouldn't be returning until Friday
evening. My parents dropped the kids off after church and the three of
them came home, excited to spend another day with their dad. School
was out and a summer full of fun was ahead of them, the kind of fun
that only kids can imagine during summer break.

That evening we ate dinner at my parents' house; Dad was outside
barbecuing when we arrived.

"Everything going okay at the house?" he asked with concern as I
climbed the stairs to the deck.

"Everything is going fine." I decided I wouldn't mention the basement monster situation.

The boys began playing baseball in the yard, and Lydia went inside to be near her grandma because she always liked helping her cook. I was sitting on the deck swing, enjoying the beautiful summer day.

"Come on over here. I want to ask you something, and I don't want the kids to hear," Dad said as he flipped the meat he was grilling. He stared at me with concern in his eyes, and I wasn't at all sure where this was headed.

"Now, I really don't believe in these sorts of things, you know?" He turned the hot dogs he was grilling for the boys. "But that thing I felt there yesterday got me to thinking." He closed the lid to the barbecue pit, still holding his huge barbecue fork in the other.

"You don't think you rented a haunted house, do you?"

I didn't know how to respond to a question like that. "Dad, I'm sure there's some easy explanation for the lights and the electricity. We just haven't figured it out yet is all," I said, trying to assure him that everything would be all right.

"I'm sure you're right. But it was the weirdest thing I ever felt before in my life. I don't know. Maybe the house is too close to overhead power lines or something. You hear about stuff like that all the time," he said, taking a sip from a can of soda.

"Are you done with that meat yet?" my mother called from the big double doors that led to the deck.

"Five more minutes is about all that's left," he called back.

"Don't burn it this time," she replied with a smile on her face.

Dinner was great. It was a typical summer barbecue meal for the LaChance family. Matthew ate too many ears of corn, and I worried about the effect they'd have on his stomach. Mom said the meat was burnt. Dad claimed it wasn't.

"Besides, Geri, the kids like it that way," he said.

"You say that every time, Freddie," she replied back, smiling at him. The way my parents carried on between themselves made me happy. The year after my sister died, they'd hardly spoken at all. And when they did, it was in short little phrases spoken only out of necessity. My parents had been married for forty-six years, and it was clear how much they still loved each other by the tone of their voices, their lighthearted banter, and the way Dad patted Mom gently on the back as he walked by her in the kitchen. I envied their life, a life that I would never lead. They had each other to lean on during good and bad times. I had me.

After the dinner table was cleared, I helped Mom with the dishes. "Did I tell you that your brother is coming home tomorrow?" she asked as she rinsed the suds off a pan. My brother, Josh, was the baby of our family, nine years younger than me. I had always viewed my family life as two separate eras: life before Josh and life after. My other brothers were six and nine years older than me, and the age spans usually puzzled anyone who asked our ages.

"Tomorrow? I thought it was next week," I said as I dried a pan.

"No, this week. He's coming for a whole two weeks. Flies out of Seattle in the morning," she replied, rinsing out the sink while watching the kids playing in the yard.

When the house was built, she had insisted that there be a window above the sink. "I have to have something to look at while I'm standing here. I have to be able to see outside or I'll just feel too closed in," she told my dad. The real reason she wanted the window was to make it easier for her to keep an eye on all of us while we were outside. Now she kept those same eyes glued to her grandchildren.

My brother Josh was a bit of a rebel. He loved to protest. And he was always up-to-date on anything that was happening in the world. Many times he would walk by me and take a look at the tag on the collar of my shirt, or he'd look at my shoes and say, "You know slave labor made that garbage you're wearing." Despite those little digs, I always looked forward to his visits and felt a deep sadness when he boarded the plane that took him back to Seattle.

During every visit I would try to persuade him to return home. "C'mon, Josh, I miss you, and I know the kids miss you all the time. Plus, Mom and Dad aren't getting any younger, you know?"

Josh would just smile at me and head for his plane—backpack slung over one shoulder, his guitar case in his hand. My heart would always drop to my stomach and my throat would throb with emotion. One last wave and he'd be gone. But now he was coming home again, and I was feeling the upside of those feelings. I couldn't wait to see him.

"Don't let Matthew eat this all at once," my mom said as she handed me a care package of leftovers for home. We both knew that Matthew would have it eaten before bed, but I guess there was always hope. Matthew was always growing and always hungry. I smiled at her with a parental conspiratorial grin, gathered the kids, and headed for home.

It was just starting to get dark when we pulled up to our house. As usual, the lights in the house shone brightly from the street. The kids were on the porch the instant the car stopped, pushing each other back and forth the way kids do, fighting for position to be the first one through the front door. As I walked up the concrete steps with the house key in my hand, ready to unlock the door, I glanced up at the second-story windows that peeked through the leaves, and for a brief moment I thought I saw someone spying on us from above. I blinked and looked again, but there was no one there. *What an imagination*, I thought to myself. Dad had really messed with my head when he asked if I thought the house was haunted.

After feeding Matthew a few of the leftovers from Grandma's, we settled into the living room to play a game. While the kids decided which game to play, I stood looking out the front window. An elderly woman was walking down the street, and like so many people before her, she crossed to the other side of the street when she reached our yard. "Let's eat some ice cream," I said, completely forgetting about the continuing ritual I had just witnessed. And completely forgetting that I had just fed Matthew leftovers not even a half-hour ago.

Lydia got out the bowls and Michael had the spoons in hand as I scooped the chocolate ice cream into the bowls. As usual, Matthew was first in line and announced, "Last one finished has to kiss my feet." This was also a usual occurrence, and to date no one has had to kiss his feet because of course Matthew never finishes eating.

Anyone peeking into our kitchen window would have seen a typical American family sitting at the table, bantering back and forth. As we were soon going to learn, however, we weren't so typical. A loud crash interrupted our ice cream party, quieting us in mid-conversation.

"Those boxes you've stacked up really need to be emptied, guys," I said after a moment. Lydia giggled nervously as she rinsed her bowl in the sink.

"Okay, rinse your bowls and meet me in the living room. I'm ready to kick some Monopoly butt," I said, running to the living room. It was way past their bedtime, but what are summer vacations for?

It wasn't long before the game board was set up and the kids were arguing over which game piece they wanted and who could be trusted to be the banker, a job that Michael always insisted should never be Lydia's.

I noticed it first out of the corner of my eye, just a quick flick of movement, something in the doorway that led to the family room. I looked toward it again and realized that it wasn't something; it was the dark figure of a man backlit by the light from the kitchen. He was solid in form, except his form seemed to be made up of moving, churning dark gray and black smoke or mist. I looked down at the game board, certain that when I looked up again it would be gone. I was tired, I told myself; my eyes were playing tricks on me. I kept trying to rationalize what I had just seen, but I couldn't. When I looked up again, he was still there. And to my horror, he began to move toward us. He came slowly at first, but then he picked up momentum. He moved into the family room and paused in the center of it. His form was still a churning mass of blackness. I couldn't see his face, but I could feel his eyes watching me, staring directly at me, challenging me. He stood in the center of the room for what seemed like an eternity but was actually only a few moments. Then he melted from sight. He was gone.

I could barely contain the panic I felt inside. What should I do? I could grab my kids and we could run out of the house in the night like the crazy people depicted in horror movies—the ones that are always "fact-based"—or we could get up and quietly leave the house to figure this out without creating a scene for the neighborhood. I opted for the second choice. We would calmly but immediately leave the house.

My hand was shaking uncontrollably as I picked up the car keys. Thankfully, they were on the coffee table right in front of me. In my nicest, calmest, daddy-has-everything-under-control-voice, I stood up and said, "Let's go get a soda and visit Grandma." Of course the boys began to groan and moan because they were really looking forward to playing the game.

Lydia, sensing something was wrong, shot me a puzzled look. Then she looked to my right hand, which was shaking as it held the keys. She looked me in the eyes, and that's when it hit her that something was terribly wrong. "Come on, guys, I'm thirsty," she said in her calmest big sister voice.

"Come on, guys. It'll be fun." The boys didn't need any further encouragement, but I could tell that Lydia was still trying to figure out what was going on. I was locking the front door when a loud, painful, tortured, agonized scream came pouring out of the house. *Our* house! It was the voice of a man screaming in pain, and it was so loud that the neighborhood dogs began barking in response.

"Get in the car! Get in the car!" I cried at the kids, who were already out the door in a dead run to the car. Michael, leading the pack, jumped over the hood of the car, a move he would later claim he had learned from a James Bond movie. I was in a panic. I knew we had to get away from that old white house *now*. I started the car, and the engine quickly came to life. The tires squealed as my shaking foot hit the gas pedal.

We were safe.

Then Matthew's frightened voice came from the back seat. "Daddy, the basement monster is standing in the upstairs window."

I looked back and there it was; the black form was standing in the window watching us leave.

"Daddy, it's in the window. It's in the window. Hurry!" Lydia urged fearfully as we rounded the corner onto the road that would lead us to the safety of my parents' house.

The drive was a blur as thoughts raced through my mind. What could that smoky apparition have been? And the scream, what was in the house that could summon up such an awful wail? What was the thing in the window? Had we really just seen Matthew's basement monster? My whole reality and my closed-minded perception of the world crashed down around me as I searched for a logical explanation for what we had just witnessed.

Thankfully, my parents were still up and in the kitchen. Dad had just taken the trash out, and Mom was readying the coffee maker for its morning brew. She was filling the pot with water as I opened the door. Without a word on my part she knew something horrible had happened.

"What's wrong?" she asked, bracing herself for the worst.

Fighting back tears, I said, "I think my house is haunted." I had been witness to what had happened, but my words sounded absurd even to me.

Dad turned to look at me. "What happened?"

"I saw it. Dad, I saw it. It screamed at us."

The worried looks on my parents' faces deepened as I told them the story.

"I knew it," my dad said.

"It was watching us from the upstairs window as we drove away," Lydia added tearfully, her fear obvious in her voice. My parents looked at me, hoping this wasn't true.

"It was. It was watching us." My head slowly fell to the table as the truth closed in on me. My father placed his strong hand on my shoulder, just has he had on the day of my sister's funeral.

"Here, drink this," my mother said, handing me a glass of water. "You need to calm down before you go into shock." Dad's hand still gripped my shoulder.

"What am I going to do?" I asked my parents, still shaking.

"You'll stay here tonight," my dad replied calmly. "In the morning we'll go over and try to figure this out."

15

The next morning I woke up in my parents' peaceful home. I lay in bed, thinking and listening to the comforting songs of the birds perched outside the bedroom window. Everything here was so normal. And yet despite the warm morning sun streaming through the window, I felt a chill run through me. I couldn't shake the vision of the shadow man. Matthew's basement monster was real. Tears filled my eyes as I thought about Matthew. I had always told the kids they could tell me anything. Matthew had tried to, and I let him down. That was one of the hardest parts to deal with. The knowledge that I let Matthew down still haunts me.

"What's wrong?" Matthew asked, wiping the sleep from his eyes.

"I'm sorry, son. I'm sorry I didn't believe you about the basement monster."

Matthew wrapped his arms around my neck in a gentle hug. "It's okay, you didn't know," he said. His sweet voice nearly convinced me that it really was okay.

Downstairs I could hear my mom moving around the kitchen. The aroma of freshly brewed coffee filled the air. My body relaxed slightly, and the memory of the previous night eased. Maybe in the heat of the moment I had just overreacted.

My father poked his head in the bedroom door. "What kind of cereal is it going to be this morning, Matthew?" Matthew bounded out of bed and headed for the kitchen to see if he could find any of his favorite chocolate-chip cereal. Michael rolled over, still half asleep.

"Is it morning?" he asked.

"Yeah, son, it's morning," I said with a grin, getting up myself to head downstairs for a cup of coffee and a bowl of cereal, if there was any left after Matthew finished eating.

After the breakfast dishes were cleaned up and everyone was dressed, my parents, the kids, and I headed back home. It was a beautiful day, and the clear blue sky made the strange events of the previous night slip even further away.

Pulling up in front of the house, I stared at it. It was just a house, a perfectly normal house like every other one on the block. Who would have guessed or understood the terror we had felt the night before? I could barely understand it myself. The house seemed harmless until I stood on the steps leading to the porch. I could feel it watching me from the window above, its eyes peering out at my family and me. I took a quick glance upward, but there was nothing there. Even so, my hand trembled as I put the key into the lock.

Inside, everything seemed normal and quiet. Nothing had moved, nothing was out of place. The only evidence of our quick departure was the Monopoly board still resting on the coffee table. All of the lights were still burning, but that was because we had left in such a rush, wasn't it?

"Seems quiet," said my dad from the doorway.

And then, from right above us, we heard a loud *BOOM*.

"Did you hear that?" was the only comment he could spit out.

"Maybe there's a wild animal trapped in the house, and it knocked over a box," suggested my mom, trying to keep our amateur investigation under control.

"Maybe you're right," my dad said as he cautiously stepped farther into the room.

Mom, Dad, and I searched the house as a group, going from room to room. There was nothing hiding in the house and no evidence of a wild animal. We switched the lights off to mark the rooms we'd searched.

"You've *got* to come see this," called Lydia. "C'mon, you guys! Come see what's in the shed!" she said as she ran back outside.

The shed was very old. If someone tried to put a date on it by its appearance alone, it would have been much older than the house. The door was standing wide open, and Lydia and the boys stood in its doorway pointing at the shed's contents. "Look at all this stuff!"

They were right. The shed was full of boxes upon boxes filled with birth and death certificates, pictures on top of pictures, photo albums, and mementos from family vacations. It didn't take long for us to realize we were looking at the personal belongings of more than one family, and not the types of things people would leave behind unless they'd left in a hurry. Whole lives were laid out before our eyes.

Mom grabbed my arm. "Steven," she said, "I think it's time to call this Mr. Winters and find out what's going on here."

She was right, and I headed inside to call our landlord. I had the phone in my hand when I noticed a large picture sitting on the floor, one that had been hanging on the wall just moments before. Now it was on the floor, leaning against the wall as if someone had taken it down and placed it there with great care. It was a picture of my daughter, a picture of Lydia. My stomach suddenly queasy, I turned my back to it and quickly dialed Mr. Winters.

It was one of the most uncomfortable phone calls I've ever made. The phone had barely rung twice when I heard Mr. Winters' voice. In my mind I could see his lips forming the word *hello*. I could hardly believe my own voice when I finally asked him if the Union house was haunted.

"Why, no, not that I recall. Why would you think it was haunted?" He meant for the tone of his question to be comforting, but it only convinced me that he was lying.

I told him what had happened the night before. I told him about the personal belongings we had just found in the shed. I told him everything.

"Now, I, myself, have never *seen* a ghost, but I do imagine it would be a frightening thing to see. I do recall being told once that ghosts are always around us. Perhaps you just tuned in to them, if just for a moment?" His odd reply confused the situation even further.

"Oh, and the items you found in the shed belong to a girl who used to live in the house. Oh my, I've been trying to get her to pick them up since she moved." Mr. Winters' explanation didn't do much to ease my nerves. After I thanked him for his time, I hung up more puzzled than I had been before I dialed his number.

I was just steps away from the phone when it rang again. It was Mr. Winters calling to say he had just remembered that some of the boxes in the shed belonged to man who had once lived in the house. He was pretty sure that he was a drug dealer.

"Yes! He got up in the middle of the night and left everything behind. *I* think he was running from the police or maybe other drug dealers. You know how those people can be."

I hung up the phone and laughed. Mr. Winters was clearly out of his mind. He wanted me to believe there was a drug ring headquartered in this house. I started to walk away from the phone and it rang yet again. It was Mr. Winters, and this time he was offering advice.

"I don't know much about these sorts of things, you know, but if you'd like I could have the house blessed. Better yet, I could call Saint Louis University and see if they would send down one of those priests that dealt with that exorcism. You know the one. They made a movie about it. An experienced priest like that would know just what to do. *I* know. I'm a Charismatic Catholic, and we do believe in spirits and such."

On and on he went. He told me about the people who had lived in the house before us. They had been living in sin. Perhaps their sin had brought evil spirits to the house. He was sure they practiced witchcraft.

"They used to burn a lot of candles. *Too* many. Do *you* like to burn candles, Mr. LaChance?"

I sighed deeply and admitted that I did burn candles, but I burned them for atmosphere, not to perform spells. "Please don't call a priest, Mr. Winters. I just wanted to know if anyone else had experienced anything strange while living in the house."

"You know, there *was* this one girl who claimed that her dead father would come and visit her at night. Maybe you saw his picture and death certificate in one of the boxes in the shed. Other than that little incident, I can't recall any others. I guess in a way you *could* consider the house haunted. Let me call a priest and call you back."

I interrupted him before he hung up and convinced him that I didn't need or want a priest. Thanking him again, I hung up, lingering by the phone and waiting to see if he would call back. But it appeared that he had said his piece.

After we tired of looking at the boxes in the shed and we had gone over the house, I packed for my trip to Indianapolis the next day. The kids got their clothes, and we were ready to go back to my parents.

"Maybe after you take a few days away from it, you'll be ready to go home," Mom said, trying to make light of the situation.

Maybe she was right. Maybe with time and distance I could make sense of the situation. The last one out of the house, I grabbed my bag and closed the front door. As I put the key into the lock, the shade on the door moved aside as if someone was peering out at me. With a shudder, I hurried to lock the door and we were gone.

16

How many times a day do you succumb to rationalizations, telling yourself that things will be just fine? You put your children on the school bus in the morning, telling yourself that they will make it to school safely. You get on an airplane, rationalizing that the plane won't crash. You rent a home. True, the odds are slim that your children will be in a bus accident or you'll be in a plane crash. What, then, are the odds of moving into a haunted house? I would have thought that the odds of us moving into a haunted house were about the same as us dying in a plane crash, and if someone were to ask how I rationalized the situation I now found myself in, my reply would be, "Just enough to make it through each day sanely." Everyone should understand the value of a good ol' rationalization.

My trip to Indianapolis was completely normal. Working during the day kept my mind off events at home. At night I had plenty of time to rationalize the whole mess. It was a one-time occurrence, I told myself. There was a logical explanation to it. It won't happen again. By the end of the week, I decided that we would go back to the house.

Friday finally arrived, and I caught an early flight from Indianapolis to St. Louis. I was back in Union by three o'clock, two hours before rush hour, which put me in a good mood. If we were going back to the house, I wanted to make sure we arrived before dark.

Besides the kids, my brother Josh was at my parents' house when I got there. We spent the evening catching up with each other. He had been in numerous protests since I had seen him last, including the big World Trade Organization protest in Seattle that filled the national news for days. He had also been through an earthquake, a bad relationship, and a thriving career in the techno music scene, where he was recognized as a great composer. On and on we talked about this and that. Finally, the discussion turned to the house. "What are you going to do?" he asked with a tone of deep concern in his voice.

Taking a deep breath, I said, "I'm taking myself and my kids home to our house. What other choice do I have?"

And that's what we did. After the dinner dishes were done, the kids and I left for home. Matthew was reluctant. "Do we have to?" he asked, hoping he could talk me out of it.

I gave him an encouraging smile and nodded. "We'll be fine, Smelly."

The drive back was too quick, and as we gathered our thoughts and psyched ourselves to go back inside, we sat in the car and looked at the house. In the evening light it looked like a great place to live.

The kids seemed to settle back into the house quickly. Maybe Mom had been right; all we needed was a few days away from the place. Even I had almost forgotten that horrible night. The evening passed without incident, and the four of us slept in my bedroom again.

Saturday was busy. We went shopping, hit a movie, and had dinner out, so we were fairly tired when we got home. It had been a great day though, and we had really enjoyed each other. We went to bed early that night, and I fell asleep as soon as my head hit the pillow.

Sometime during the night, the nightmare came to me for the first time. Later I would realize that it was always the same. The same darkness. The same sounds. The same stairs. The same fear. Maybe I wouldn't have been so frightened if it had played out like a story with a beginning, a middle, and an end. No, this nightmare picked up in the middle of the story. My dreaming screams would wake me up, and I would be left with shattered shards of the dream . . .

It's dark. I'm standing on the basement steps. They're old, wooden, creaky, and worn. Flowered neon-print wallpaper is peeling off the walls of the stairway. It's barely visible in the moonlight cast through the basement windows below. I grasp the handrail and steady myself; calming my nerves, I begin my slow decent into the moonlit darkness below. The stairs seem to go on forever. With each step I hear a familiar creak that announces my progress.

I hear water running, and I'm going to investigate its origin. A few steps more and I see a candle burning. It gives off a warm, dim glow. There is an unattended lit candle in the basement . . . this is only a dream? Yes? Dismissing the candle from my mind, my attention turns to the sound of the rushing water, and along with the water I can hear breathing. It's the labored breathing of a man; he is excited, perhaps even sexually excited. I turn back to the candle-light. The old butcher shower is running. A man stands beneath it, showering by candlelight in the darkness of the basement.

The water and the breathing echo throughout the basement; the man doesn't see me. I watch as he tries to cleanse himself, purify himself of a dark substance, scrubbing his already raw skin. His face is hidden by the shadows. His labored breathing becomes panicked as does the pace of his scrubbing. He can't get clean.

He turns. I can see his frontal torso in the light. It's blood, he is washing off blood. Is he looking at me? I can't tell in the dim candle-light, but I sense his evil eyes on me as he continues washing.

The room begins to spin. The sound of his desperation matches the tempo of the rushing water. Still the room spins, spins, spins. I can still feel his eyes on me. I can't breathe. Oh my God, I can't breathe . . .

I woke up with a start, trying to catch my breath. *It was just a vivid dream*, I told myself. I looked to see if I had disturbed any of the kids. They were each sleeping soundly, and with relief I lay back and was instantly asleep again.

I heard the noise of a distant lawnmower before I opened my eyes. What time was it? I had to get the kids ready for church. Mom and Dad hated it when they had to wait for them. My eyes began to focus; was that a five I was seeing? No. No way. It couldn't be. The clock read 5:05 p.m. Had we really slept seventeen hours? It might not have been so unusual for me to sleep that long after a business trip, but not the kids. The latest they ever got up was noon. I didn't take any more time to figure it out. We had to get up and get going, because we were already five minutes late for dinner with my parents.

17

Mom's Sunday dinners were always great. Of course, this one was extra special because Josh was home. She had prepared all his favorites: fried chicken, mashed potatoes and gravy, and a nice salad. No matter whom we invited over for dinner when we were kids, if we had fried chicken, they would always ask to come back the next time my mom made chicken. There were leftovers, which Mom sent home with us.

Matthew clutched the package all the way home. "Dad, do you think I could eat some of this chicken when we get home?" We all smiled because it didn't matter what I said; later one of us would find him with a drumstick in his mouth. "I'm hungry!" he would protest.

It was Sunday night and we were all settled in for the evening. The kids had gone into the bedroom to play. Both bedroom doors were open, the one at the bottom of the stairs and the one that led out into the living room. I could hear the kids as I sat relaxing in my chair in the family room. It was one of those rare evenings that single parents get to enjoy, quiet and peaceful. I heard Lydia walk into the bedroom where the boys were playing and say, "I'm going to read in here while you play, okay?" Both boys mumbled in agreement. It's the last thing I heard as I dozed off in the comfort of my chair.

The ringing telephone cut through the silence. It rang maybe two times before I answered it. It was my mom, reminding me not to let Matthew eat all of the leftover chicken in one sitting.

As we chatted, I heard the doors rattle. Not the outside doors, but the ones inside. I listened more closely. They rattled again. I yelled at the kids to quit playing games. Everything was fine, I told Mom, just the kids playing tricks. Again the doors rattled, but this time a little bit harder. I scolded the kids, telling them to behave. Then, as before, the doors rattled harder, but this time before I could say anything, Lydia's scared voice cut me off. "Daddy, that's not us. I'm reading and the boys are asleep."

The rattling grew louder, and as my daughter spoke I felt the temperature in the house drop instantly. A bolt of electricity shot through my body, accompanied by a horrible stench. Then the screaming began; it started softly, then built to unbearable decibels. Through the noise I heard the bedroom doors slam shut. I didn't understand what was going on, but at that moment I knew I had to get to my kids, my kids who were closed off from me by the slamming of the doors.

My mother was still on the phone, and by now she could hear the screaming. "Come help us, Mom! Please, come get us!" As I dropped the receiver, the whole house began to shake as it came to life. Boom. Boom! *BOOM!* The screaming continued, and through it all I could hear Lydia's screams. "Daddy! Daddy, what's happening?"

I remembered that one of the two bedroom doors connected to the second floor, where I had seen the peering eyes and the basement monster. If it was coming downstairs, I had to get to my kids. In the seconds that had ticked by, the whole house had come alive with noise. The floor beneath me shook as I made my way to the opposite bedroom door. I could feel something behind me, and I knew I didn't want to turn around to look at it. BOOM! More screaming, this time that of a child. BOOM! SCREAMS! BOOM! I made it to my bedroom door, but it wouldn't open. I knew the door wasn't locked because the hook and eye lock were on my side of the door, and the hook was dangling idly on the doorjamb. By now my own screams added to the cacophony. I threw myself against the door, but it didn't budge. Again and again, I pounded my body against the bedroom door but it didn't move.

"God, please! Please help me!" I prayed loudly, and just that quickly the door fell open. Michael took Matthew by the hand, and they ran out the front door to the car. Lydia was in shock and I couldn't get her to move; for the first time in her life, I slapped her. Thankfully, she responded and I was able to grab her hand and lead her through the open bedroom door. The door closest to the stairs slammed open behind us. It was on our trail and I couldn't let it reach us. I didn't turn around to see what was coming after us, but I could feel it closely on our heels.

All the while the house continued its macabre activities. BOOM! SCREAMS! BOOM! SCREAMS! Lydia and I reached the front door and met the boys at the car. From the street and the relative safety of the car we could still hear the house alive with its noise. I drove to the top of the hill, where I parked to wait for my parents. As we waited, we watched the house. Whatever was in the house was searching for us. We could see its blackness move from room to room, searching carefully, methodically. *Oh my God*, I realized. *It was looking for us.*

Finally, we saw the thing melt away into the kitchen; it was gone and the house stood silent. My right side was bruised and throbbing from throwing myself against the door. The boys were silent, shaking. Lydia softly cried.

"Why us, Daddy? Why us?" she asked.

"I don't know, baby. I just don't know."

A knock on the driver's side car window made us all jump. It was my dad. He spoke quickly, frantically. "Is everyone okay? Is everyone all right?" Just the sight of him brought all my emotions to the front.

"I think I'm losing my mind," I said to him, hoping he would reassure me that I was fine.

"No, son, you aren't losing your mind. These things just happen sometimes," he said with his ever-steady hand on my shoulder. His assurance then turned into determination. "Let's go figure this out." And with that, we were on our way back to the house.

The troops had arrived.

18

The children sat in the car, watching as I walked back into the house with my parents and my brother. I opened the door slowly. There was no need to unlock it; in my rush to leave the house I hadn't locked the door. My only thought had been to get us out of there. The living room was still, quiet. The entire house was quiet. No sound. No movement. Complete silence. The cordless phone was still on the floor where I'd dropped it.

"It seems too quiet . . . " My mom's voice broke off and I turned to look at her. Her face was ashen white and tears were streaming down her face as she stared at her arms.

"What is that?" she asked quietly.

Somehow, that short sentence gave me a tiny sense of relief. I had another witness to some of the madness my little family had been experiencing. "That's that electrical feeling I've been telling you about."

A serious look of determination came over her face. "My grand-children aren't coming back into this house." With that she left the house.

"I have to pack up some things," I said, heading to my bedroom, my dad and brother in tow. As I started gathering clothes, we heard movement and whispers from above. The three of us ran up the steps to the room that was to have been the boys' room. This was where the noises had come from. I opened the door. There was no one there. There was nothing moving. The room was completely silent. And then we were overcome by a putrid smell that caused us to cover our mouths and noses.

From downstairs we heard the voice of my sister-in-law Rita. "Are you guys in here?" she called from the living room. "Your mom left to take the kids home," we heard her say. Rita was a kind and gentle soul. It didn't surprise me to see her walking into the house. Through the years she had become somewhat of a surrogate mother to my children.

My dad said, "Things seem pretty quiet right now. We heard some movement and whispering from upstairs . . . " His voice broke off at the sound of a young girl's scream.

I was standing next to Rita. We stood silently, listening to the scream. That's when I noticed it for the first time. Breathing. Heavy, labored breathing. "Rita," I whispered, "hold your breath a moment." Tears began to roll down Rita's face. It was apparent the breathing wasn't coming from either of us, but from between us.

"I think we've had enough for the night. Get your stuff, Steven, and come on." My dad clearly wanted to get out.

Dad climbed into his truck. My sister-in-law, who now believed all the stories she'd been hearing, was heading to my parents' house as well.

I paused on the porch with my brother. "Hold on, Josh, I have to lock the door." Josh was standing on the porch directly under the canopy of the two very old trees that shaded the walkway. We heard a rustling in the tree branches above us. Peering into the night sky, we tried to see what was moving above us. Josh looked at me and whispered into my ear, almost whimpering, "They're in the fucking trees."

I nodded. Josh looked up as a shadow dropped to a lower branch as if to take a better look at us. The tree limbs shook as it dropped. With this my brother screamed, "Run! Run!!" We heard something drop from the tree as we ran to the truck. We didn't look back to see what it was, but whatever it was, it was after us and getting closer.

"Go! GO! They're *coming after us!*" Our voices trailed off as we drove away. Away from that house, away from that nightmare.

When I was finally settled in my parents' house between my two boys on a fold-out bed, I decided to call Mr. Winters in the morning and tell him that I'd had enough of his crazy house. I wanted out of the lease, and I was determined to do whatever it took.

Sleep came slowly that night. Every sound in the house disturbed me, as if there were something sneaking through my parents' house searching for me. When sleep finally did overcome me, the nightmare came, too, just as it had come before.

The same darkness. The same sounds. The same stairs. The same fear. Once again his shadowed face appeared to look in my direction. I could feel his eyes on me as he desperately tried to wash away the blood. The room began to spin, the sound of his desperation matching the tempo of the rushing water. Spinning. Spinning! I could feel his eyes on me. I can't breathe! Oh my God, I can't breathe!

I sat straight up with a yelp. Sweat covered my body. My breathing came heavy and my heart pounded. The two boys on either side of me stirred slightly, but they didn't wake up. I lay back down, staring at the ceiling for what seemed like hours. I tried to get straight in my mind what was happening to my family. There had to be answers, and tomorrow I was going to get them from that old man.

19

The phone rang several times before Mr. Winters answered it. I didn't give him too much room for comment as the story came flowing out of my mouth.

"I would *so* like to speak with you about this in person if I may?" I heard him say on the other end of the phone.

Jesus Christ, I thought. *What more do we need to talk about?* My family and I were attacked last night. Attacked in the house we rented from him.

"Let's say we meet at the house around one-ish today?" he persisted.

Okay, I thought. *If he wants to meet me at that damn house, we'll meet at that damn house.* I fervently hoped he would experience whatever was going on there so I agreed, hanging the phone up angrily. Mom raised a questioning eyebrow at me.

"I'm meeting the old man at the house." With that I turned from the kitchen and went to get ready.

It was another beautiful summer day. A gentle breeze blew, and the sky was clear and blue. I arrived at the house at exactly one o'clock. Mr. Winters, of course, was almost an hour late. As I was unwilling to go into the house alone, he found me sitting on the front steps when he arrived. I noticed he had a very large woman riding with him.

Getting out of the car seemed to be quite a struggle for both of them; the passenger huffed and puffed as she made her way onto the pavement. She weighed at least three hundred pounds and was wearing a flowered muumuu that almost perfectly matched the neon flowered wallpaper on the stairway to the basement.

As usual, Mr. Winters was attempting to exit his vehicle while clutching his wig to his head. The breeze didn't help his situation, and it caused the wig to slide down his nose. His lips pursed together as he hoisted himself from the car. If my situation hadn't been so awful, I would have been laughing hysterically as I watched them.

"Mr. LaChance, how nice to see you again." Mr. Winters walked toward me, his smile reaching me before his outstretched hand. "It's *such* a fine day for an outing that I thought I would get my dear friend Lillian out of the home and bring her with me." Lillian was still standing by the car, holding on to it as she regained her breath and steadied herself.

"We don't have long to stay, you know. I have to return Lillian to the home very soon." He made a little loopy gesture with his hand, leading me to believe he was referring to the nut house.

There wasn't anything I could say in response to his comment so I glanced down at the pavement. There were Mr. Winters' feet. They reminded me of the scene in *Cinderella* in which the wicked stepsister tried to force her foot into the glass slipper. Just like the stepsister's foot, Mr. Winters' feet bulged over the tops of his shoes.

Heavy breathing approached us, not from house this time but from Lillian, who was finally making her way to the steps where we stood. After what seemed like an eternity, we were up the steps and at the front door. I invited the two of them into the house, offering them a seat.

"Oh my, it feels so nice and cool in here," Lillian said sweetly as she plopped onto my expensive couch that I prayed would hold her.

With pride, Mr. Winters replied, "New insulation." He then turned to me and said, "*I* have never heard anything about this particular house being haunted. And I, myself, don't really believe in ghosts and such, but I do notice, Mr. LaChance, that you seem to burn a lot of candles, which has led me to wonder: do you practice *witchcraft* here in my house, stirring things up and such?"

"Oh my!" Lillian gasped again.

"Yes, Mr. Winters," I began, tying to stifle my mounting anger. "Yes, I *do* like candles. What I don't think is that it means I'm into witchcraft. You're using candles as an excuse to explain why your house is haunted, which I think is deceitful."

Lillian spoke up at this point. "You know, I've heard stories about an Indian chief haunting this land here." Mr. Winters glared at Lillian. "Well, it *is* one of the stories I've heard, Carl. You know that. You've heard them, too."

Mr. Winters shifted in his chair to look his friend in the eye. "I hardly think any of those old wives' tales have anything to do with this house. I've been sitting here for many moments now, and I've felt nothing odd."

To my surprise, Lillian turned and looked me straight in the eyes. "That charged feeling you sometimes get when you move around the house?" I nodded in shock; how did she know about that? Had Mr. Winters told her? Lillian simply laughed. "Well, that's your ghost, honey. I felt it as soon as I walked in the front door."

Mr. Winters immediately got down to business after that comment. The only way he would let me out of my lease was if someone took it over from me; he might even have someone already. I wasn't sure how I felt about the whole business. I was angry that I couldn't just walk away from the whole mess, but there was a part of me that understood he needed to have the rent paid by someone. In any event, it sounded like he was going to do the footwork for me.

"I have a cousin who is looking for a place. This just might be a great solution for you and for her as well," he went on to say.

Then a new thought hit me. How could I let another family move into this nightmare without any forewarning? On the other hand, it *was* one of his relatives.

"Mr. Winters, this isn't the type of place you want to rent to people with children." The least I could do was to make that one of the stipulations of our agreement. Smiling at me, he agreed. "Of course not. I certainly wouldn't want any more little angels in this awful situation." We shook hands and they left to wedge themselves back into the car.

The transfer of the lease took a little longer than I'd hoped. In the meantime, we lived with my parents. I'd just returned from a business meeting in Buffalo when I learned that Mr. Winters' cousin would indeed take over the lease at the end of July. It was happy news for me, but I was still angry that I was paying rent for a house that we couldn't live in. My only comfort was that I knew other children wouldn't be moving in, and I could now begin finding a new place for us to live.

Ultimately, I settled on a duplex. It was new and completely modern, with a full basement and an attached garage. I think its newness was the main attraction. It would be a house without a history, and safe for me and my family.

20

Moving day finally arrived, and I rented what seemed to be the same truck we'd used just a few months earlier. The large dinosaur captivated Michael again as it rolled into my parents' driveway to pick up my dad, who was going to help me with the move. I had to explain to the kids why they couldn't come help us move out of the house, but I assured them that I'd pick them up as soon as I could and they could help unpack at the new house.

"Ready for this?" I asked my dad.

"Ready as I'm ever going to be," he replied as he backed the truck out of the driveway.

In a very short time we pulled up in front of the house. I had tried avoiding it as much as possible. Once a week I stopped by to pick up the mail, and at those times I left the car running with the door open.

I'd run up to the porch and back to the car as fast as I could. Those brief contacts had been tough for me, but now Dad and I were going to have to spend several hours in there getting all of our belongings packed up and out of there.

If there was any luck in the whole haunted-house mess, it was that we hadn't unpacked everything. Dad and I worked quickly, removing box after box. We had most of the items moved out of the downstairs when the pounding began again on the second floor. Boom. BOOM! Dad looked at me with fear in his eyes.

"Ignore it, Dad, just try to ignore it." But instead of me trying to ignore it also, something snapped. I wasn't going to take it anymore. I was ready to fight back. At that moment I ceased to be the victim. I became a survivor. Determination surging through my veins, I walked to the bottom of the stairs and yelled, "You won. Do you hear me? YOU WON. We are moving out. I am getting us out of here and away from you. DO YOU HEAR ME?" I punctuated each word with a pound on the stair rail. "Now, if you keep this up and make this harder on me, I will find a way to make you burn in hell forever. Do you understand me?"

I'd had enough of the bullying. It wasn't going to do this to me when I was trying to get out. And it didn't. The house remained completely silent as Dad and I finished the move. About four o'clock, Mr. Winters drove up.

"Hello, Mr. LaChance. I'm supposed to meet the *new* residents here. Have you completed packing your belongings?"

I confirmed that we were finished and would be pulling out very soon. I glanced at the street, where a car was pulling up to the curb. In it were a man, a woman, and two small children. I could barely contain my rage as I looked at Mr. Winters. "You said that . . . "

He cut me off mid-sentence. "Aren't they the sweetest little angels," he said as he walked away from me.

I looked at Dad helplessly; I felt I needed to do something. As he always did when I was upset, he put a steadying hand on my shoulder. He said, "Let's go, son. We're finished here." And so we left.

We parked the truck outside the new house and drove my car back to my parents' house. Mom fed us a quick dinner and then the kids and I headed to our new home.

"My room is the one upstairs across from Daddy's," Lydia said, immediately staking claim to her kingdom.

"Go ahead and take it. Matthew and I are getting the entire basement as our room." Michael taunted her. Before things could get out of hand, I reminded him that they would only have the finished part of the basement.

The sun was just beginning to set when we pulled into our new driveway. I knew we'd have to work pretty fast to get the majority of our belongings inside before nightfall. I had just opened the back sliding door on the truck when I heard, "Mr. LaChance! Mr. LaChance! I just knew this is where you meant when you said a 'duplex just up the road.'"

It couldn't be, but it was. Sweat poured down his forehead from underneath his wig. It was Mr. Winters.

"Mr. LaChance," he chided me in a painfully playful manner. "You forgot to leave your keys to the house. I hope you don't mind that I stopped by to get them." He paused for a moment looking over our new home with an appraising eye. "My, this *is* a nice place. Nice and *new*." His voice lingered on the word *new*. "You know some people simply aren't meant to live in an old house and everything that comes with them. I just think you are one of those people."

With that, I handed him the keys and he was on his way. I hadn't said as much as two words to him. As he drove away, my daughter looked up me. "Oh, Daddy. How did he find us?"

I gave Lydia a reassuring smile and shrugged my shoulders as we continued moving in our things.

As it got dark we stopped working so we wouldn't disturb our new neighbors. Before going to bed I took a hot shower, standing under the rushing water and letting it unkink my knotted muscles. What felt even better was that I didn't have to watch for something joining me there. After our showers, the kids set up their mattresses in my room. We would bunk together for at least one more night. I wasn't sure if it was for the kids' sake or for my own, but I felt it was the best way to get through our first night in our new home.

It was nice being together because we wanted to be, not because we were afraid to be separated. We kept the hall light on for comfort as we talked and laughed. Finally, I settled the kids down with the reminder that Grandma and Grandpa would be picking them up for church in the morning. We'd settled down into our pillows and blankets and were dozing off when from the kitchen came a loud crash. The children screamed, but I began to laugh. It was fresh ice tumbling into the bin in the freezer.

"It was just the icemaker, guys. No bogeyman this time." Rolling over, I fell into a deep, peaceful sleep. It was great. But then the nightmare from the house began again. *Spinning! Screaming! Blood! Staring!* I was sitting straight up when I woke up. It was already morning and time to get the kids up for church.

"Get 'em up! Get 'em dressed! Get 'em clean!" I yelled, jumping out of bed in my usual fashion, shaking off the dream. It was new day, and a new life lay before us.

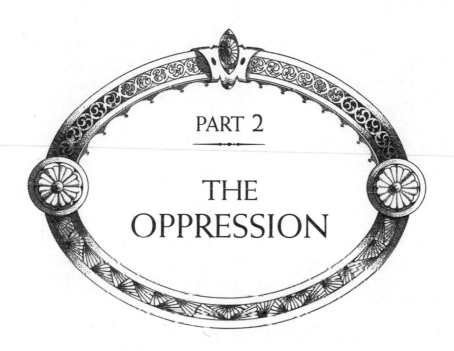

PART 2

THE
OPPRESSION

21

You know how life goes. A minute turns into an hour. An hour turns into a day. A day becomes a month. And a month becomes three years. Before you know it, you're staring backwards and wondering where all the time has gone. This was much the way the years passed for me after we moved from the Union house. Instead of counting minutes, hours, and days, though, I was counting sleepless nights. Nights usually plagued by nightmares.

"Mr. LaChance." I came back to the present; the sleep technician was talking to me. "We're going to have to shave this small portion of your hair in order to completely attach all of our electrodes." The room was cold and sterile, and I was wondering how in the world I was supposed to sleep in such a place. The sleep study was my parents' idea. Well, theirs and our family doctor. I suspect they may have been discussing my nightmares behind my back.

"Mr. LaChance?" the technician said again.

"Oh! Of course, cut what you need to get it done," I replied. "It's only a little bit of hair."

I think my family thought I'd lost my mind. Almost immediately after moving out of the house, I fell into what I thought was a deep depression. I was still highly functioning, but I was always extremely fatigued. I felt like something was literally sucking away my energy. I could hide it at work by scheduling myself at odd hours. Most of the time that worked, and when it didn't, I'd make the necessary excuses to make it all right. This sleep study was actually the last in a series of tests. I'd already gone through a battery of tests, including a stress test and a CAT scan; the results from all of them were normal.

"Are you completely comfortable, Mr. LaChance?" With my nod, the technician turned out the lights. "I will be monitoring you in the next room. If you need anything, all you have to do is ask." I knew that a tranquilizer was absolutely out of the question. The technician left, gently closing the door behind him. For the first time in months, maybe in years, I was lying in a bed in complete darkness. I hated the darkness. "Don't panic," I told myself, repeating it over and over. I finally decided to close my eyes so they'd adjust to the darkness more quickly. "Mustn't panic, Steven," I told myself. For some reason, it hadn't crossed my mind that I'd be expected to sleep in a completely dark room. I heard a noise; it sounded like something was being wound, maybe gears turning. When I opened my eyes, I could make out a single red light on a video camera. The lens was churning back and forth, trying to find the right focus to record me as I slept.

"Don't panic," I muttered to myself. Since living in the Union house I hadn't been able to sleep in an unlit room. The darkness seemed to move. I didn't know how else to explain it to people. The darkness moved for me, toward me. *"Don't panic, big guy!"*

Then another thought crossed my mind. This would be the first time in three years that I was going to be able to sleep without worrying about anything. The kids were safe with my parents, who would watch over them like twin guardian angels. I was at the diagnostic center with someone who would watch over me as well. Let the technicians earn their keep. With that final thought, a sense of calm came over me and I fell fast asleep. I hadn't slept that well in years.

The sleep test revealed that I suffered from sleep apnea. I actually stopped breathing once every minute, which kept me from going into any type of deep REM sleep.

"What about my nightmares?" I asked my doctor.

The doctor looked at me, puzzled. "Nightmares?"

I was sure we'd found the answer to my nightmares. "Is the sleep apnea causing my nightmares?"

The doctor took a deep breath and looked me directly in the eyes. "No, Mr. LaChance, with this type of sleep deprivation you should not be dreaming at all. No dreams. No nightmares."

22

I kept my bedroom window covered at night. I'm not talking about covering the windows with the decorative curtains most people have in their bedrooms. Mine were covered in three layers so that not the slightest bit of light was able to penetrate its protection. Protection? Protection from what? From another of the many nightmares I'd been burdened with since we lived in the house? I don't know. I'd like to think it was simply my overactive imagination. Over the last few years, though, life had taught me that it's fraught with many possibilities. My dream life began soon after we moved into the new house. I'd wake up in the middle of the night, and I'd swear that something was standing just outside my window, watching me from far enough away that I couldn't see it or make out its face. Still, I could feel it watching. At first I thought we had a nosy neighbor, maybe the perverted type who got sexual kicks from watching others sleep. Night after night I experienced the same sensation of something peeking in at me. One night I actually got up the nerve to jump out of bed and push back the curtains. There was nothing there. Nothing, yet I was sure that I saw it standing. Standing? Standing where? I didn't know, but I knew it was standing right outside my bedroom window, watching me and waiting for me. Waiting for what was the unspoken, unanswered question.

One night I went to bed so tired that I could hardly stand. I was working too many hours, and I needed to get some sleep. Just as had happened other nights, I was awakened by the familiar, eerie feeling of being watched. I sat up in my bed. For the first time, I could actually see my watcher and it was moving closer and closer to my bedroom window. I thought I could make out the form of a man. I rubbed my eyes. Was it a man? He, it, gained momentum as it came toward me. Was I filled with fear? Yes, I was filled with fear. Every fiber of my body pulsated with it. I was an over-tightened guitar string, and if the thing I was watching came much closer, I would snap. Blond hair . . . yes, I could see that my watcher had blond hair. It came still closer to my window. I could see his eyes when he paused right outside my window. His eyes seemed to glow in the light of the moon. They were white, stark white. No pupils, no iris. I wanted to scream, but I couldn't. I wanted to run, but I was frozen, caught in the spell cast by my watcher's lifeless eyes.

The sound of shattering glass brought me back to my senses. He was climbing through my window. A huge smile revealed pointed teeth. His white eyes danced with menace. He was in my room and I could clearly see him. He was a demonic imitation of a man. Another scream built in my throat as he came toward my bed. Finally, I began screaming. He reached for me, but I jumped from the bed and pushed him aside as I raced for my bedroom door. He was on my heels. Someone was grabbing me. Holding me. Stopping me. Oh my God, he had me! The sound of my own screams filled my ears, and I could feel his breath on my neck.

"Daddy! Wake up! Daddy, please! Wake up!" My vision cleared, but I was still resisting, trying to get away. "Daddy, wake up. It's only a nightmare!" It was Lydia, and we were both terrified. "It was only a nightmare, Daddy," she repeated soothingly over and over.

Only a nightmare? It was another remnant left over from the terror we'd lived through at the Union house. Why wouldn't the demons of the past go away? Why couldn't I leave this behind? Let it go? Or was *it* not able to let go of me? I was frozen by the possibilities for new horrors that this new thought hinted at. And now there was this new nightmare, a nightmare when the doctor said there shouldn't be any. I needed to get this out of me; I needed to put this to rest.

It was exactly three o'clock in the morning when I began writing about our brief life in the Union house. At four o'clock, I was done. It wasn't a complete telling, but it was close enough. I stared at the computer screen. I'd put this nightmare on paper; now what was I to do with it? Then it hit me. I wanted to share my story with others. I'd spent the last three years of my life reading what others had to say about this sort of thing. Now I sat at my computer and stared at the screen. There it was: my story. More than anything I wanted to share it with someone else. Maybe I could find one more person who felt as scared and vulnerable as I did. It took an hour to post my story in a few places on the Internet, where I hoped it would be found by someone who understood what I was going through. Exhausted, I went back to bed.

By the time I sat down at my computer to check my e-mail, I'd almost forgotten the events of the night before. I looked at my inbox, and then I had to look at it again. Over one hundred e-mails were waiting for me. Each of them had questions about my story.

I'd always felt that the Internet wasn't the best place to do research. Let's face it, most of the information on the Internet is slanted to one point of view or another. And the paranormal websites were no different. What I found was that there were many different ways of looking at the paranormal on the Internet. Some people believed that hauntings couldn't hurt you. Some believed they could. There were some who believed that ghosts were simply lost souls. And there were the extreme few who believed all ghosts were demons. However, as I sifted through all of this information and asked myself what my beliefs were and how they'd changed, I came to an understanding of what I thought to be true. In the coming months I found that those beliefs would be tested time and time again.

The Internet offered me many opportunities to connect with others and share experiences, and I found myself fascinated with the strange social experiment known as the paranormal chatroom and forum.

That was how I met Sheila, through a paranormal forum. She sent me an e-mail asking if she could drive by the Union house and take some pictures. I'd heard that Mr. Winters had turned the house into a dog kennel, so I thought there'd be no harm.

Nothing could have prepared me for what was to come. Nothing could have prepared me for the nightmare that was continuing within the screaming house even after I'd left it. What I thought was a journey's end turned out to be only a beginning. That's how I met Sheila, and because of her I was about to meet Helen.

23

One Sunday evening late in May 2004, three years after my family and I moved out of the Union house, my phone rang. "Steven, this is Sheila. I got to Union about two o'clock. I followed your directions exactly, but I got really confused when I got there because I couldn't find a dog kennel. There was a lady standing in the front yard of what I just knew had to be the house. Well, I stopped and I walked up to her, told her that I was looking for a white house in the neighborhood that I'd heard was haunted. Steven, she looked at me and said, 'You must be talking about my house. My house is haunted.' I thought I'd just die right there. I asked her if I could take some pictures, and she said it was okay.

"Steven, there are two children living in that house. One boy that I saw, and the woman said something about a girl. I told her about you, and I told her where to find your story so she could read it for herself."

I couldn't believe what Sheila was telling me. The house hadn't been turned into a dog kennel. There was a family living there. Worse, there were two children living there. Choking back my fear at the thought of the children, I asked, "Did you get her name?"

"Yes! Her name is Helen. Helen March. And if you get something to write with, I'll give you her phone number. She wants to talk to you. She said tomorrow morning would be great."

Myriad questions raced through my mind. Would this woman think I was crazy? Was she experiencing the same things my family had? Were her children being terrorized the way mine had been? Suddenly, the significance of my phone call with Sheila hit me. There were children in that house. I had been gone from it for three years, but in that instant I knew I had to go back. The house was drawing me back. And I began to shake.

24

Like my own, Helen's life had not always been an easy one. Frankly, life isn't all that easy for any of us, but Helen had made all of the classic mistakes. In fact, she had been wrong so many times that in her later years she found it nearly impossible to make even the simplest of decisions.

In the early 1970s, Helen had left her father's house for good, clad in a pair of jeans with a Beetle Bailey patch sewn on the back pocket. Much to her mother's dismay, the patch depicted Beetle sporting a huge marijuana leaf as he flashed the peace sign. Helen was getting out of her parents' house, and to her all that mattered was her freedom. She didn't understand yet that she was jumping out of the frying pan and into the fire, and that her freedom would come with a heavy price tag.

Like Helen's father before him, Helen's first husband was an abusive alcoholic, and she found herself hating him for it. Helen herself had never been much of a drinker, and it took her many years to get over her father's illness.

Just a kid herself, Helen was a single mother of three girls and had no place to go, but she found work with the state and realized that she enjoyed working. Over time, Helen climbed her way up through the prison system—first as a guard and eventually as a prison-guard trainer. She'd always had a soft spot for kids, however, and held on to the hope that one day she could work with them. When there was an opening in the juvenile correction system, she jumped at the chance.

Helen and her kids settled into a comfortable life, and she became the neighborhood mom. Hers was the home where all the kids congregated, and she was the kindhearted woman they went to when they were in trouble. Even after her children were grown and gone, this remained true. A mother to anyone who needed one: that was Helen.

Helen had already raised two of her daughters, who were out on their own by the time the third daughter was nearly ready to leave home. Then Helen met Charlie, a truck driver. He, too, was divorced, and his four children were already on their way into adulthood when he became involved with Helen. Charlie was black, and Helen, with her shocking blonde hair, couldn't have looked more German had she tried. Things had never been easy for either of them before they met, but together they felt a wholeness they'd never experienced before.

Charlie was middle-aged and Helen almost there when they married and were blessed with a daughter, Kelly. She was a bright-eyed, beautiful, happy-go-lucky child. The giddy couple felt like they had been given a second chance at life and happiness. Their life together was simple, uncomplicated, and they liked it that way.

One snowy afternoon Helen had a nasty fall on the steps in front of their house. She cracked a few ribs, but the real damage was done to her foot. Several surgeries were performed in an attempt to repair it, but it would never be the same. Helen had to give up her job with the juvenile court system, which she would always regret. And thus, disabled for years while she rehabilitated, she became a stay-at-home mom with her energies completely focused on her daughter, her home, and the neighborhood kids who deeply loved their surrogate mother.

One of the hardest things parents have to do is watch their children make many of the same mistakes they did. Helen and Charlie both had children who were doing just that. Helen had Patty, a headstrong girl who always did exactly what she liked. Just as Helen had done before her, Patty married young in order to escape her mother's house. And as Helen had also done, Patty jumped into her own personal hell. Three children and many beatings later, she left her abusive husband to move in again with her mother.

Charlie's son, Jared, had a drug problem that was causing his health to fail, and Charlie worried about him constantly. Charlie had seen drugs take down many men before, and he didn't want to watch his son go down that same road. Jared's crack addiction was getting him deeper and deeper into trouble, however, and with each dollar he spent and each pipe he lit, the addiction took weeks off his life.

So there they were. Helen and Charlie had a teenage daughter, two older children in trouble, and they were all living together in a trailer. In addition, Patty had one of her children living with them. Her other two children lived with their father. There simply wasn't enough room for six people to live in one trailer, so Helen began looking around for a new place to live. She thought a house would be nice, but she didn't get her hopes up. She was surprised and excited, then, when she came across an ad in the newspaper about a house for rent:

Three-bedroom house for rent in Union. Full in-town living. Near most schools and the city park. Perfect for families. A full country kitchen with up-to-date amenities. Large living and dining area with original woodwork intact. Two bathrooms with mudroom. Full basement with fruit cellar attached. Large front porch and backyard perfect for children. The right house at the right price for the right family. If interested, please contact . . .

Helen just knew this was the house she was looking for. She immediately picked up the phone and dialed the number in the ad.

A man's voice answered the phone on the other end. "Hello, this is Mr. Winters . . . "

25

Early one morning a few days after Sheila contacted me, I decided to call Helen—after sitting on the couch and staring at the phone for a few minutes. I have to admit I was a little worried that she would think I was crazy. *Think*? I knew she would think I was crazy. Sheila had told Helen where to read my story on the Internet, though, so I knew Helen would already have an idea of what had happened to my family and me. But I wondered if I should just forget the whole thing, act as though I had never heard of this woman, and move on with my life.

Then my thoughts turned to the children living in the house. Could I turn my back on them and still live with myself? If I did call Helen, what did I think I could do to help her? On and on my thoughts raced until finally I put them aside, and with one deep breath dialed the phone.

Helen answered the phone almost immediately. She had been waiting for me to call and couldn't wait to talk to me. She had many questions for me, but first she wanted to tell me her story, her story of what it was like to live in that house. I couldn't believe what I was hearing.

"It amazed me how closely your story resembled what happened to my family when we first moved in: the way Mr. Winters showed us the house like it was a museum, the smell of fresh-baked cookies when we walked in the front door. The open house he held. Like you, I remember thinking that I just had to get this house. It took him about a week to call and tell me we were getting the house. But this is the strange part. He also had me meet him at a restaurant to sign the papers, and he insisted that the walk-through take place during the day because he said he didn't like to drive at night. He seemed very jumpy when we were in the house, very jumpy. He's not normal, that's for sure."

Helen continued comparing our experiences with the house. Her daughter Patty had only lived in the house for a short while and was terrified the whole time. Charlie's son didn't spend very much time there either and, unfortunately, died a few months after leaving the house. Helen now lived in the Union house with her husband, her teenage daughter, and her grandson.

Then she began to tell me about their experiences. She would hear someone breathing right next to her when she was in the house alone. They would hear footsteps above them and sometimes hear footsteps coming down the stairs and into the bathroom. Naturally, when they investigated, no one was there. The hair was cut off her daughter's dolls, something Kelly promptly denied doing herself.

Each occurrence was more disturbing than the last. "I took my granddaughter upstairs to show her a kitten we just got the other day. It was horrible, Steven. When I went into the bedroom I found the cat dead on the floor. Its neck and back were both broken. I got my granddaughter out of the room so she couldn't see it, but it was horrible."

I couldn't believe the things I was hearing. It was clear that the house was still very active. And I have to admit that I felt a perverse sense of relief; it wasn't just me these things had happened to. It wasn't just my family. It was happening to someone else as well.

Helen went on. "I was home alone one night last week. The kids were at my daughter's house spending the night, and Charlie had to work late at the nursing home where he does maintenance. In the middle of the night came a knock on the door and it was the police. They told me a suicide call had come from my house. I was the only one home and I sure didn't make it."

She had other stories to tell me, too, about things that hadn't happened to us. The gutters on the house were constantly catching on fire. The transformer in front of the house blew up every few months. She had heard whispers and seen things move. She was constantly replacing light bulbs, and the most recent event had her very worried.

"My grandson said something pushed him down the steps. I found him at the bottom of the stairs pretty beat-up and bleeding. He's going to go live with his father. I need some help here. I'm afraid this house is going to hurt one of us if I don't find some help soon."

Charlie, she said, thought she was crazy. It was a relief for her to talk to someone else who had lived in the house and experienced his own mysterious anomalies.

"You know, every time I leave the house I feel as if someone is watching me from those upper windows. And I never know what I'm going to find when I come home—the lights all on, doors open, windows open."

What seemed like a short call was actually over two hours long. We agreed that the best thing we could do was to try to find some history on the house, so we arranged to meet at the library the next day to see what we could find. We had no idea we were about to open a huge can of worms.

26

At the library we didn't find out much about the history of that part of Union. The librarian was less than helpful, and at times it seemed she was racing ahead of us to remove materials from the shelves so we couldn't see them. "The old wives' tales about that part of town being haunted are just that, old wives' tales," she snorted at us when we tried to explain to her why we were looking up the history of that part of town. Her voice stuck in my mind as we moved on: "old wives' tales . . . old tales."

Our next stop was at the courthouse to look for deeds. Each time we left an office, the workers would call ahead to our next stop to alert them that we were coming. For whatever reason, it seemed they were hiding something.

Eventually we learned that the Union house was built from a Sears kit sold through that company's catalog. The railroad had dropped it off at its location in 1936. The history of the land was far more interesting than the history of the house itself, though. In fact, the entire neighborhood had an interesting story. The land had been part of the property of an army officer, Captain John T. Cromwell, and the Union house stood right where Captain Cromwell's slave quarters had been located. Another house directly across from the Union house on the next street had once been known as the "murder house." In 1971, a woman murdered her husband there and then took her own life. On another corner was a big gray house where a man had shot himself to death in front of his young son, not more than five years ago.

The nursing home on top of the hill in the park connected to the land had actually been an infirmary during the Civil War. After the war it became the county poorhouse. When people died there, often from tuberculosis or another horrific disease, they would be buried on the property in unmarked graves. This meant that the whole area was essentially one large, unmarked mass gravesite.

The most colorful background belonged to Captain Cromwell. An officer in the Union Army, he started the first Missouri Militia in the Civil War and was also the town's sheriff and judge. He was a 33rd-degree Mason who not only had the respect of the town but also held all the power, too. He lived on the property with his second wife, Minerva. Cromwell was also the head of the town's morals committee, which was responsible for passing judgment on any townsmen who committed transgressions. Stories of his exploits were many. One story had him lining up four hundred Confederate soldiers and executing them. By the time he was done, the town was covered in a thick blanket of smoke. Six Union soldiers were murdered on his land by Confederate soldiers in retribution for mistakes made at the Battle of Pilot Knob in southeastern Missouri. No one is sure why they were brought back to Union for execution, and anyone who did know never revealed the motive. Cromwell was indeed a powerful man—a powerful man with powerful friends.

It was rumored that a tunnel system ran from somewhere on the Cromwell property to a location at the bottom of the hill. Some speculated that it might have run to the train tracks, where slaves could have been shipped in for sale. It seemed that Cromwell had been part of the slave trade and the railroad was used partially for this endeavor, but no written history has ever been found that could confirm this rumor. There have only been the whispers of the town's old historians, who always cautioned that this was secret information that should not be discussed. Some thought Cromwell might have been a Southern sympathizer. Not that he actually sympathized with the South; he just hedged his bets so that no matter how the war turned out he would continue to profit. That is perhaps why the Confederates brought the Union soldiers from Pilot Knob to execute them on Cromwell's land. Again, that's speculation on the part of a few of the town's old folks. Sometimes in a small town certain things are just better left alone. Thus, Captain Cromwell's shady past remained mostly unstudied.

Yet the tunnel system did turn out to be fact. A street crew dug into it one day when they were replacing some pipes. Maybe it had been weakened by the raging runoff waters of the flood of years ago. Of course, the tunnel system was immediately filled in with bricks and covered back up. It remained another tidbit of information about Union and John Cromwell that would never be investigated. Maybe it would bring up too many questions, and "they" wouldn't want that to happen. That's the way it is with small towns in the Midwest; some things are better left alone.

People whispered about Cromwell's involvement with his slaves and with voodoo. Others claimed that he made a deal with the devil and sold his soul long before his death. When people in Union talked about him, it wasn't out loud in mixed company, of course, but in whispers. The townsfolk so feared him that they only engaged in whispered suppositions that Cromwell had either been in cahoots with the devil or that the devil had taken him over. There were other whispered rumors about a hanging that took place on the Cromwell estate. It seemed that the captain "took care of" those people who stood in his way. Maybe not immediately—but eventually and always, anyone who crossed him met an untimely (and probably painful) death.

Then there was the story of the large Indian chief who lived on the Cromwell land for a very short time. It was Cromwell who gave the order to execute him. There were further rumors about a Cromwell friend who provided abortions to the whores of Moselle, and the rumor whispered about the abortion given to Cromwell's wife Minerva when she became pregnant by a slave.

Were all of these rumors just the folklore of a small town? When old tales like these circulate long after the events they describe, there is usually an element of truth to them.

27

After five long years of pledging allegiance to the propeller clown hat, I found myself out of work. Why? That's what bothers me, the "why" of why I lost my job. I hadn't done anything wrong. As a matter of fact, I lost my job because I did the right thing. But as the company managers put it, I lost my job because I had become a "liability." I had promoted a truly qualified woman who deserved the promotion after her years of dedication. But my actions weren't favorable to the image that the company wanted to give to its clientele.

You have to understand that in this part of Missouri, folks of color can work in food courts and sweep up after shoppers, but to get a position in one of the prestigious stores was unheard of, let alone a promotion to a managerial level. I had tested the old boys' network, and now I had to pay the price. I was unemployed and the woman was demoted. She filed suit. In the end she was paid $35,000 in damages, plus the back pay she should have received from the moment I promoted her.

However, I was out of a job, and I couldn't find one anywhere. The harder I looked, the tougher the job market became. It was almost as though there were forces conspiring to keep me down. At times I wondered if there was something that didn't want me to work, that didn't want my attention diverted to anything positive. I know now that I was the mouse in a game of cat and mouse. The cat was a demon. Then, however, I had no idea what was happening. I just knew there was something terribly wrong.

*   *   *

Helen's luck wasn't any better. She was worried her family was falling apart. Her grandson had moved out of the house. Her daughter Kelly had long shown signs of trouble and now began cutting herself. Often girls will do this in the hope that the pain they inflict on themselves will mask other problems in their lives. In Kelly's case, we would eventually learn that she had begun hearing voices that told her to hurt others, to kill others. She cut herself with the hope that her self-sacrifice would appease these voices. But we had no idea then what was going on with her. How could Helen, Charlie, or I even imagine something like that was happening to her? Kelly was also skipping school, and Helen was sure she was using drugs. Helen began to attribute her family's problems to the house, and since it had been Helen's decision to rent it, the thought that she had done anything to harm her family was depressing her.

"Steven, you wouldn't believe Kelly's mood swings. Of course the doctors want to medicate her, but no one wants to tell me what's going on with her," Helen told me one day over the phone.

"Do you want me to help you find help for this haunting?" This was the first and the only time that I would ask Helen this question.

"Yes!" She replied quickly. "We need help."

Every major American city has one: a house or hotel that's advertised as haunted. Usually such a place is touted as one of the most haunted places in the country, and St. Louis is no different from any other city in this respect. It has a haunted mansion built by a family that ran a once-popular brewery. The brewery became very successful, and with its success came unbelievable wealth for the family.

The mansion was built on top of a series of caves and caverns, which helped add to the legend of its secrets in later years. Radio-show hosts clamored to broadcast from the mansion on Halloween, and promoted contests to see which listeners could spend the night there without packing up and leaving before dawn. Thanks to all the hype, of course, rarely did any of these people stay in the mansion all night. This particular haunted mansion had a horrible past. Almost every member of the family that lived in the mansion committed suicide. Many people in St. Louis felt that the family had been cursed. Even the family dog succumbed to the ruthlessness of the place. The dog's owner shot it right before he turned the gun on himself, the gunshots echoing through the mansion and the caves and caverns below.

Where does one find help for a haunting? We thought this mansion seemed like a perfect place to start. I already knew that a psychic gave ghost tours there every Monday night. Her name was Betty, and I found it very easy to make contact with her. She suggested that Helen and I come to one of her tours, and afterward we would sit down and discuss ways to get Helen's family the help they so desperately needed.

Early one Monday evening I picked up Helen, and we set off for the city and the haunted mansion. When I pulled up in front of the Union house, I honked the horn and waited for Helen to come out to greet me. I simply wasn't ready to go back inside that house.

On the way into St. Louis, it was obvious we were both nervous about what we were getting ourselves into. We made small talk about the places we passed, but we spoke very little about the Union house or the meeting we were going to. When we got to the mansion, visitors were already gathering in front, waiting for the tour to start.

The front door opened, and we filed in through the very large front doors. In the vestibule I saw a small middle-aged woman with shocking red hair. This had to be the famous Betty whom everyone had told us about. I introduced Helen and myself. Betty told us to go ahead and enjoy the tour and afterward we would talk.

The group was first escorted into a huge dining room, where we were given liability waivers to sign. Helen and I glanced at each other nervously as we signed the waivers.

The tour lasted about two hours. It was mostly a history lesson about the house and its previous occupants. Betty made a couple of attempts to contact the dead on the way up the stairs. Helen and I both agreed that we felt and saw nothing—until we entered the attic. There Betty told us about the family's son who was born with severe Down syndrome. The boy was locked in the attic, where he lived until his death.

Betty asked everyone to turn off their flashlights and stay very quiet while she tried to make contact with the dead. It was obvious we were in for some type of séance. A candle was lit in the center of the room, and Betty began speaking to the spirits. As she talked the room got very cold. Then, very close to the floor, about the size of a dog, a white, glowing, foggy light floated into the room. I looked at my feet as it passed in front of me. The girl next to me turned on her flashlight, which upset Betty very much. She declared that her concentration had been broken and the tour was now over.

After the others left, Betty sat down and listened to our stories. Could she help us? She would try, but she told us she would need to visit the Union house. We settled on a date that suited all of us. Betty looked me squarely in the eye and said, "You need to be there too, Steven. It's time for you to go back and face your fears."

Helen and I were quiet on the way home. As I drove I wondered how I'd get up the nerve to go back into that house. Suddenly Helen giggled, and then laughed. "They call *that* house one of the most haunted places in America? Just wait till Betty sees my house." Then we both laughed because we knew it was true. Betty was in for the shock of her life.

28

The evening of the first Union house investigation was finally here. Helen and I decided that I should arrive a little before Betty so I could get through my first moments back inside the house.

I took a huge breath as I pulled up in front. For a moment I sat there and couldn't move. Thoughts went rushing through my head. *What in the hell am I doing? I must be out of my mind going back into that place.* My heart was beating out of my chest.

I looked up at the house. It seemed so innocent. Not in the least the monster I remembered. The rationalizations had already started. *It'll be okay. Nothing is going to happen. We have a professional coming.* I sat there and remembered Lydia's face in the window as I left home, her telling me, "Be careful, Daddy." I had to do this. I had to do it for myself, and I had to do it for my children. I took a huge deep breath as my sweaty hand reached for the car door.

I eased myself as I took my first steps onto the stairway leading to the front door. Finally reaching the door, I rang the bell. A few seconds later Helen was there opening the door, inviting me into the all-too-familiar living room.

"I'm back," I said jokingly as I entered. Helen's husband Charlie was also there. We spoke briefly, and he made it clear that he felt we should just leave well enough alone. "I have to tell you two, you're messing with something here that my mother always told me to leave alone. If you aren't careful, you'll find yourselves in something you both can't handle." Charlie had been raised by a very old-fashioned mother full of warnings and superstitions. Who could blame him? It wasn't that he didn't believe in ghosts; it was *how* he believed in ghosts. Charlie felt that the spirit world should be ignored even if it came bounding onto your front porch. That's the way it was with Charlie, and that was the way it was with his mother. Some things were just better left alone. Charlie excused himself with a shrug and a sigh. Kissing Helen lightly on the cheek, he headed to work.

Betty and her male assistant, Lee, arrived right at eight o'clock. Betty already appeared winded from walking up the stairs to the porch. "There is something that does not want us here. I can feel its resistance," Betty pronounced from the front door. Helen and I glanced at each other, wondering what would happen next. As Betty entered, she told us that she and Lee were going to walk around and get a feeling for the house. She asked Helen and me to show them around.

We started on the main level. I found it difficult to focus on the present; my mind couldn't help but flash back to my personal experiences in the house. Then we started walking up the stairs. Betty paused halfway up the steps, and Helen and I were sure she had felt something. We went through the boys' former upstairs bedroom toward the breezeway at the back of the house. Betty walked ahead of us, and that's when we felt it.

Both Helen and I felt the force as it rushed by us in a cold burst of energy. We turned to look at Betty and knew instinctively that the force was headed straight for her. A second later Betty was lifted about three inches off the floor and thrown against the wall. Helen and I gasped in horror as Betty tried to regain her composure. "You two better wait downstairs," she told us. She didn't need to tell us twice before we headed back to the main level. Sitting in the living room, we listened as Betty and Lee moved quickly through the house. They had electromagnetic field (EMF) meters that screamed at the heightened energies they came across. The meters screamed ceaselessly when Betty and Lee entered the basement. After some time they both came back upstairs to the living room.

Betty told us they had come across the spirit of a man upstairs. He made it clear to her that this was his house and he didn't like having people live there. Then Betty became even more serious when she spoke about the basement. "There's a vortex in the basement where spirits can freely come and go. Sometimes something very bad can come through these vortices. It's possible that something of this nature may have already come through this vortex. It's a very powerful opening. It isn't my place to tell you to move, but if you continue to live here you need to try to avoid that area as much as possible."

That was the full extent of Betty's comments before she and Lee left. Helen and I looked at each other, more confused than we had been before their visit. We never saw them again. Neither one of them ever returned to the house. Helen and I were on our own again. On our own again, left to deal with and make sense of it all.

I was excited when I got home that night. All three kids greeted me at the door, their eyes full of questions. I sat down and told them what had happened and everything that Betty had told us. Lydia gave a big sigh of relief. "Maybe now people will believe us?" It was a question that hung in the air then and still hangs in the air today.

29

The first time I heard about the baby hanging in the tree I thought Kelly had lost her mind, another victim of the Union house. She was clearly excited when she called me early one morning. She was frightened and obviously upset as she spoke.

"Steven, you'll never guess what happened last night. I was sitting on the porch talking on the phone with one of my friends when I heard something in the tree to my left. I told my friend I'd see what it was and call her back. First, it was a black shadow that seemed to move through the tree very quickly. Then I heard it crying." Kelly was speaking very quickly and I was trying to make sense of what she was telling me.

"A baby, Steven! I heard a baby crying, and when I looked over at the tree there was a baby hanging by its feet, wearing a white dress. I screamed. I mean, I couldn't believe what I was seeing. I ran inside to get Mom, but when we went back out it was gone."

Helen took the phone from Kelly. "Steven, she swears she saw it. I've never seen her so upset. She's very frightened."

The only thing I knew to do was wait until dark and then go over and wait to see what might happen. The kids would be all right that night with my mother. I told Helen I'd be over as soon as I could that evening, and we hung up the phone.

Charlie was working the night shift, so it was just the three of us at the house. Kelly was still talking a mile a minute, and I hoped that she would calm down with me there. Helen and I sat on the front porch for what seemed like hours. In the distance the sky lit up, indicating a thunderstorm on the way. Flash, light, then dark. Flash again, light, then dark. The rumbling thunder was now audible in the distance.

We sat there waiting and watching as the storm approached. The wind picked up around us and the lightning got more frequent. Flash after flash lit up the scene for a moment and then plunged it back into darkness. The treetops above us began rustling, the sound nearly muffled by the impending storm. At first the rain fell gently—drip, drip, drip. Then there was another jolting bolt of lightning and we both saw it. Hanging in the tree, lit only by the blinking flashes of lightning, was a baby. It hung upside down by its feet and wore a christening gown. The gleaming white gown glowed brightly in each flash of light. The child was clearly dead as it swung there from the tree. Then the wind picked up around us. The lightning flashes blinded us with their frequency, and it felt like they were arrows aiming for us but missing their targets. We stared in horrible fascination at the dead baby hanging in the tree. Shock quickly took us over. We couldn't speak and we couldn't move. We just watched it in the tree swinging. Swinging by its feet. Finally, we could take it no longer. With the storm still raging around us, we ran inside for shelter.

Helen looked at me, her helplessness and disbelief palpable. "She did see it, Steven," she whispered. "Yes," I replied, frightened to the point of being breathless. "Oh my God, Steven, what was that all about?" Helen began to cry. "I don't know, Helen. I just simply don't know anymore." I tried to stay calm and brave, which at the moment was very hard because my heart was pounding in my throat.

The storm's fury lasted for about half an hour and eventually turned from an angry torrent to the nice, soft pitter-patter of a summer rain. Helen opened the side window in the family room, which faced the tree where the baby had been hanging. The baby was gone, and there was no sign it had ever been there.

From the street we heard someone humming, followed by the "tap, tap, tap" of footsteps playing in the rain. The humming continued; it was the voice of a child—soft, cute, young. It wasn't a familiar tune. It was the tune a child might make up as he played alone, the song of a ghost child.

Helen leaned toward the window. "Oh my God, Steven, do you hear him?"

Yes, I did. I pressed my face to the screen, but I could only hear him playing. I couldn't see him. I spoke to him, "Do you wanna come and play?" I could hear him giggling and the tap, tap, tapping of unseen feet going by in the dark. I spoke again, "Do you wanna come and play?" Silence. Even the humming stopped.

Then violently, viciously, a low guttural growl came ripping through the window from outside. It sent me reeling back in terror. Never before had I heard anything like it, and there was no mistake it was angry. I sat down shaking.

"I don't think I'm leaving you tonight," I said, when I managed finally to speak. What could I do? I couldn't leave them alone in the house without Charlie. I couldn't leave them alone with whatever angry thing was lurking just out of sight.

None of us slept that night. I think Helen, Kelly, and I felt we might never be able to sleep again. I stayed awake with them. When Charlie arrived home from work at five in the morning, I went home, exhausted and very confused.

30

It is impossible to understand the psychology behind a haunting, or why events can be violent one day and as innocuous as the sounds of a child playing the next. I only know that each event is like a snow-flake, different in its look, its presentation, its feel. This was the case with the Union house. There never seemed to be rhyme or reason to its madness.

Helen was beginning to look tired. Each time I saw her she would appear more tired than the last time. Her smile wasn't quite as bright as it used to be. There was an underlying desperation taking over our conversations as events in the house escalated.

"Steven, could you come over? There's something in the house growling at me, and it's coming closer and closer."

I made record time getting to the Union house that night. I could feel the electrical charge as soon as I reached the front steps, and I knew something major was happening inside. I could feel it and I could smell it; the foul odor of rotten flesh that was often present greeted me even before the door was opened.

Helen was clearly shaken. "It started very softly, and then it just kept getting louder and louder and closer and closer."

She had barely ended her sentence when I heard a loud, animal-like growl emanating from another room. I knew that sound. I slowly moved toward the room. Scared out of my mind with pure adrenaline pushing me on, I peeked into the room and looked around, but I couldn't find anything. I turned my back to return to Helen, and the basement door opened as I walked by it. I grabbed it firmly, slammed it shut, and locked it. Again, we heard the loud growl coming from the other room.

"Steven, what do you think that is?" Helen's body was trembling.

"I don't know, but it sure does sound pissed off," I replied. And it did; it sounded like a very angry animal. I went to the doorway of the other room and yelled, "What do you want from us?"

With this it growled again, as if trying to verbalize something. Why had I asked? The one thing I didn't want was a conversation with this creature. The basement door opened again, and I went over and firmly shut and locked it.

The growl came again, this time loud enough to shake the room. Then silence. We could hear a little bit of movement coming from upstairs and then that fell silent as well. Helen and I sat together for what seemed like hours staring into the other room, waiting. But it was all silence.

Then Helen said to me, "I have to show you something. I just don't know what to think about this." She rolled up her sleeve, revealing what appeared to be a large, red, and bruised bite mark. I could see where the teeth had punctured her skin.

"It's a bite mark," I said, not even trying to hide my shock. "Helen, how did you get this? Who bit you?"

Helen could only look at me with terror in her eyes. Then, almost whispering, she said, "I don't know. It happened in my sleep. Something bit me in my sleep."

At that moment I knew we were running out of time, and I had to find help for Helen. I didn't want to risk finding out what would happen if we didn't.

31

In the coming weeks it became clear to us that it wasn't going to be easy to find anyone with the right expertise to help us. What we found instead were groups of amateurs, voyeurs, harlequins, harridans, shysters, drunks, and worse. There was no end to the "investigative" groups offering to visit the Union house. They would come in, look around, and go. Just when we thought we had found a group of people that could help us, they would leave us after gathering their evidence. There was never a lack of evidence to be had there either. These "investigators" took photo after photo, video upon video, recordings and more recordings. We were always told there was nothing in the house that could possibly harm us. Whatever was in the house was just trying to scare us. We were advised not to feed it our fear.

Each group that came to investigate the house came with their psychics in tow, and they each came up with a different cast of characters they claimed inhabited the house. First, Helen and I were told about Mary and John who had lived in the house. They didn't want anyone living there but themselves. Next we were told about Frank, who had killed Jack because Jack tried to rob Frank. Another psychic told us about Shirley, who had tried to give herself an abortion in the seventies. It was supposedly Shirley's baby we were seeing hanging in the tree. Another story involved a slave named Mack, who had tried to kill his master and his wife. Mack was allegedly hanged in the tree outside the front door of the Union house. On and on the psychic characters came and went.

They collected evidence and took it away, never sharing any of it with either Helen or me. Most of the time we never heard back from any of the groups, either. What they did leave behind were their own eccentricities that did nothing to help Helen. For example, one woman hadn't been in the Union house for more than two minutes before she took of her shoes and began rubbing her feet on the carpeting and furniture. She didn't have anything significant to add to any of the investigations other than her smelly feet.

The third group said they wouldn't be back because they had seen photos of the Union house online. They were angry that someone else was involved.

Another group came in, and one of the investigators was thrown against the wall by something unseen. They stayed another ten minutes and then left, never to be heard from again.

Then there was the investigator who persistently called Helen at four o'clock every morning to "discuss" her situation. Despite Helen's request that the investigator call her at a decent hour, the early-morning calls continued, robbing Helen and her family of what sleep they could grab between episodes. Finally, the investigator told her that the Union house was possessed by a demon. That was the last phone call Helen received from that group.

The next group didn't want to hear anything Helen had to say about her experiences in the house. In fact, they instructed her to sit quietly on the couch while they made up their own minds. "They even went through my dresser drawers, leaving my bedroom a complete mess," she told me. Unbelievably, that team also seemed more concerned about where they were going to eat than with the actual investigation at hand.

Another of the many teams that came through the house arrived with over twenty people, although they had told Helen only two people would be coming. They brought two cases of beer and various bottles of hard liquor. Two of the "investigators" sat across the street in their car smoking pot during the investigation. Later, they used "dowsing rods" to find a good place to barbecue. They went so far as to give Helen's daughter a set of dowsing rods so she could talk to the ghosts. This group concluded the evening by telling Helen the house was haunted by six different ghosts, and they gave her their names.

The next group to come in told us the house was haunted by five different ghosts and gave us a different set of names. Seven was the number the next investigative group came up with—seven new ghosts with seven new names. Helen halfheartedly joked one evening that the house must host quite a party every night.

The final and ultimate indignities involved Helen's daughter Kelly. First, two investigators ganged up on her and accused her of practicing witchcraft. When I asked them how they knew this, they said they had a "psychic impression." The second indignity came when an investigator looked around the house for twenty minutes and then advised Helen to institutionalize her daughter. This person hadn't even met Kelly, who wasn't there at the time. This investigator even presented Helen with a preprinted list of institutions.

Each group had a different explanation for Helen, none of which fit what we had experienced in the house ourselves. Through it all Helen continued to be her grandmotherly self, remaining so brave. She greeted the "investigators" in each group and welcomed them into her home with a smile, a cup of coffee, even cookies or a piece of cake. She would sweetly cooperate with them, answer the same questions over and over, and endure indelicate, probing questions posed by strangers half her age. Each group promised to stay in contact, promised to help, and promised to come back when they found a suitable explanation for the haunting and a way to end it. Always they promised, and always they failed to deliver.

Finally, Helen had enough. She had a new bite mark on her arm, and the lovely twinkle that once danced in her eyes was gone. "I've had it with these groups. I could take anyone in off the street and let them into my house, and after ten minutes they could tell me this damn place is haunted." Suddenly, Helen's grandmotherly facade cracked. "Ten fucking minutes is all it would take. I know my damn house is haunted. What I need is help," she cried.

From that moment on, things changed. We rolled up our sleeves and got down to the work of doing ourselves what needed to be done. At least that was the plan. First, we began to gather together people we thought could help. We found a psychic named Alex and his sister, a photographer named Mary. Next we met a guy, Mark, who had all types of surveillance equipment. My friend Sheila introduced Helen and me to a sensitive named Carol. All of them seemed dedicated to helping find Helen the right kind of help.

This, I thought, was the foundation of the right type of investigative group. We called ourselves Missouri Paranormal Research (MPR). We would walk to our own drumbeat. We vowed to work on a case until we found a way to give our client closure. And Helen was our first client.

32

From that point on, during nearly every moment of every day, a member of MPR stayed with Helen. She was never left totally alone, because by the end of the third month it was clear that the ordeal Helen was going through was taking a toll on her. Her health declined even as we watched her. Worse, her blood pressure couldn't be controlled. Right before some big paranormal event in the house, Helen's blood pressure would go through the roof—but her pulse would drop to forty beats a minute or lower.

By now the house always seemed ready to blow. One night Helen and I heard noises coming from an upstairs bedroom. I made it to the top of the stairs before Helen, and much to my own terror I found myself standing toe-to-toe with a large, black mist apparition hovering over my head. It was huge and engulfing. Its negativity pulsed through me, making me nauseous. I stared at the mist as it hovered around and above me.

"Steven, I think—Oh my God! . . . " Helen cut herself off in mid-sentence when she saw me in a standoff with this thing. I planted myself in its path. I wasn't backing down. I was sure it would have me if I decided to run. The only thing I could do was stand my ground and face it down. After a few moments it began to swirl, and then it dissipated until it was gone. My legs went weak. I passed out, and luckily the bed at my side softened my fall.

"Steven, you did it!" Helen's reassuring voice brought me back to reality. "You stood up to your biggest fear," she said as I shook uncontrollably.

The house continued its assault on Helen and the MPR members. We encountered hot spots, cold spots, appliances turning themselves on and off, items disappearing from one room only to reappear in another, unbelievable things.

Mark, the surveillance expert we'd recruited, is a very large guy. One night he was with a small group in the basement. He'd just checked the fruit cellar door to make certain it was tightly closed; he couldn't budge it. He turned his back to walk away when he heard the door scrape on the basement floor as it opened behind him. He turned to see a large, black-hooded figure with red glowing eyes enter the basement from the fruit cellar. It was coming right at Mark, who began screaming. He was in shock when we walked him out of the basement. Mark, another person affected for life by this house.

Things like that happened on a daily basis. Then events started to take on religious connotations. One day Helen wasn't home when her mother called. Her mother's name, telephone number, and the time she called were clearly on the caller ID. Later her mother called back and asked Helen why she had such a strange message on her answering-machine message. She said a woman had answered Helen's phone, uttered the Lord's Prayer, and hung up.

One night Helen and I were upstairs sitting in the breezeway when something very large moved by us; as it passed us, it said "Jesus" in a low, guttural voice. We didn't know what that meant, but we quickly returned back downstairs.

Day after day, hour after hour, event after event took its toll on Helen. With each passing day, she became more tired, her smile a bit more faded. She was slipping away from us, and we didn't know how to hold on to her.

PART 3

THE
POSSESSION

33

Four a.m. My phone was ringing. "Hello," I groggily answered. Helen was at the other end. "Steven? Steven?" she whispered.

"Yes, Helen, I'm here."

She was crying and clearly upset. "Steven, I think I'm losing my mind," she said suddenly. "I think I want to kill my husband, Charlie, and I'm afraid I could actually do it. I have this walking cane that was my dad's. I was lying next to Charlie in bed, and I saw it leaning against the wall and I had the most horrible thought race through my mind. I saw myself picking up this cane and smashing Charlie in the head with it. It broke his skull open. And then I thought to myself, *I could really do this*. He wouldn't even have time to wake up. I could kill him, and he wouldn't be able to stop me."

With this she started crying harder. I told her it was okay, it had probably just been a dream. I told her it was the stress she was under. I tried my damnedest to explain it away, but I couldn't. Not for her, and certainly not to my own satisfaction.

"Then last night . . . I didn't tell you this, but I woke up and Kelly was standing at the foot of our bed. Steven, she didn't look like herself. She was staring at Charlie and me. I swear she looked like she wanted to kill us. And I understand now what Kelly had to be thinking. I understand completely because I wanted to kill him, too. I wanted to split his head open with that cane. And Steven, I'm afraid that sooner or later I'm not going to be able to stop myself."

We talked for hours, trying to make sense of it all. We talked until daylight. Helen was in big trouble. If I didn't find help for her soon, someone would get hurt. Nothing, however, could have prepared me for what happened the next night.

34

Who knows why life happens the way it does? One day I was living the sweet life, and everything was just as I'd always imagined it would be. I had a wife, kids, and a job. The next day my wife has abandoned me and our children. I'm living in a haunted house. I've been fired from my job. What could I have done to have my life fall apart so quickly with no forewarning? Did I do something to deserve this? Still, my kids were my joy, and they were doing fine.

Then there was the matter of Helen. What had she done to deserve living in a house so evil that it was sapping the very life from her? Who had let loose this Pandora's box of events that now made up our daily lives, become our personal living hells, and eternally knit us all together? Why had we been selected to witness this awful dance of the demons? Had we missed a signpost or a moment amidst this madness where we could have taken another road? Neither Helen nor I had lived our lives planning for this eventuality. We had no premonition that we would ever need to prepare ourselves to fight the devil for our souls and those of our loved ones. And when one does find oneself in a battle for which rules don't exist, how can a mere mortal prepare?

Members of MPR were still staying with Helen around the clock, which was taking a toll on everyone. Alex was the strange one in the group; he was more than a little eccentric. He worked as a personal assistant by day and sold sex toys at parties by night. He claimed to be psychic. However, when I would put him to the test I found that he was no more psychic than anyone else in the group. Alex had been going through a very bad time. There are times when you instinctively pick up on warning signs. With Alex the red lights were going off everywhere.

Helen and I found out that Alex had become interested in the occult. One night I found a stack of books he brought with him to the Union house. Both Helen and I were concerned because they were books about black magic.

"It isn't black magic, Steven. I'm just practicing a little bit of gray magic."

I knew there was no such thing as gray magic. It was clear to me that he was practicing the black arts. I told him, "Take your books out of this house, and if I ever see you bring something like this here again you will be asked to leave and will not be able to return. I can't tell you what you can and can't do on your own time, but while you are here, this will not happen." I could see the relief in Helen's eyes, and Alex agreed. From that day on, though, I knew I needed to watch him like a hawk.

When I would sit down to talk with Alex about these things, he would clam up and simply state, "Don't worry about me. I can take care of myself." Unknowingly, his addictions began to get in the way of our work at the Union house. Sometimes he would seem almost out of his mind. One night he ran through the house like a madman, screaming at unseen entities, challenging them. Much later on, I found out that he'd been taking painkillers that had been prescribed for him when he'd had kidney and gallbladder problems. These pills were often washed down with booze. What worried me at that moment was that the Union house itself was becoming an addiction for him. Later I would find out that on one of his tirades one night, an unseen force grabbed him and began sexually groping him. Instead of being frightened the way most people would have been, he seemed to enjoy it.

Then Alex began telling us about the dreams he was having. Demons were visiting him at night while he tried to sleep. They were stealing his sleep away from him. He began to age; it was like watching his youth slip away from him. The house had begun to consume him.

The night after my pre-dawn conversation with Helen I was very tired, since I had been up for hours on the phone with Helen. Alex showed up at the house on one of his usual tirades, scaring a couple of Christian women who were at the house hoping to help Helen.

"Steven, I want to discuss something with you," Alex announced. "I want to perform a ritual in the basement of the house. I want to do what they call a bloodletting ceremony. I'll make a salt pentagram and stand in the center of it with Bobby, one of the neighbor boys who hangs out here. Then I'll cut myself and Bobby, and we'll bleed in the center of the pentagrams. This will bring the demons to me. I will bind them to myself and take them away."

I stared at him in horror. Alex had completely lost his mind. Nothing he could say would allow me to stand by and watch him perform this ceremony and take these demons home to his two small children. The Christian ladies were equally horror-struck when they heard the idea. Absolutely not, I told him. It was obvious to me that he was completely beyond our control.

The next thing I knew, he was asking Helen's permission to perform this appalling ritual. Helen also made it very clear that she wouldn't allow Alex to compromise her home further through such a stupid act. Alex immediately left the house that night. He was angry, defiant, and upset that we wouldn't allow him to follow through on his plan. I spoke with his sister later and advised her to find help for Alex. I said that Alex was no longer welcome at the Union house.

We—Helen, the other members of MPR, and I—made this decision in an attempt to protect Alex from both the house and from himself. The house had begun to take over Alex's life, and its influence was becoming frighteningly clear. We made this decision in order to protect him; sadly, it was a failed mission.

Within a week of my conversation with Alex, the original MPR group broke up. Alex had begun to act like a victim, as if our decision to prohibit him from entering the house or performing the bloodletting ritual in the basement had been done to harm him or his reputation. He attempted to slur Helen and me by telling people that we were crazy because we wouldn't let him perform his ritual. Sheila, Mary, and Mark also left the group shortly thereafter. They harbored grudges against me for a long time, and their public behavior had changed substantially. I have chalked this up to the house, which, I concluded, had taken three more "prisoners of war." Subsequently, Alex was institutionalized. He became homicidal and suicidal. I offered to help him find spiritual guidance, but we never heard from him again.

Clearly, the demons were free of their Pandora's box and their dance had begun. They had taken control of the house as well as those people foolish enough to let their guard down while inside it.

35

"I had two more bite marks on my arm when I woke up this morning," Helen reported to me over the phone. "I've been sleeping with my bedroom door closed and locked. I'm frightened of Kelly. There are times when I think she wants to hurt us, to kill Charlie and me. I feel so guilty when I have these feelings, but there's something to it. If things keep going this way, one of us is going to get hurt."

Helen's mood changed as she began to tell me of her dreams. "I'm standing alone in my room. It's dark and I'm wearing a black dress and a strand of white, perfectly shaped pearls. I'm dressing for a funeral. I just don't know if it's Charlie's or Kelly's. Then I realize I'm dressing for my own funeral; I'm wearing my burial dress. It's almost funny. In my dream I've never looked or felt better, and yet I'm glad I'm dead. Then I wake up.

"I swear, Steven, when I do wake up, I swear that something has been in the room with me, watching me sleep. I know it because I can smell it. Its wretched stench lingers in my bedroom. It's something evil. I know it. Steven, I need help. I'm losing my mind, and I'm afraid of what I might do without meaning to. I'm afraid I'll hurt Charlie or Kelly or myself." She was crying.

Day after day I watched Helen slip away. With each malevolent act by the house, and with each scratch or bite, we lost a little bit more of her.

Many times I told Helen that I thought she should just move out of the house as I had done, but then she'd remind me that she and Charlie didn't have enough money to move into another place. At this point, we also believed that we had an obligation to somehow stop this nightmare without putting another family through what we had experienced.

I went on the Internet. Surely I could find some help there. Then it hit me. I remembered a famous haunting case, and I searched for the man who had investigated that case and had helped the family—Ken Sparks. I would turn to him for help. My search led me to Tom Gennerra's webpage. I e-mailed Tom and he responded almost immediately, urging me to telephone his father-in-law, Ken Sparks. Ken, he said, was an angel on earth. A noted ghost hunter and demonologist, Ken had investigated some ten thousand cases.

The very next day I went to Helen's with Ken's phone number in my hand. "Here's a phone number we're going to call together. This man is one of the best, if not the best, in the field of paranormal investigation. If he can't help us, no one can."

Helen picked up the phone and dialed the number. To our surprise, Ken answered on the second ring. In a very short time, Helen explained to Ken everything that had been going on at the house, and it didn't take him long to respond.

"You have a demon in your house. You need to find yourself a good priest and get that place blessed." Ken explained to us what he meant by a good blessing, the procedure that the priest should follow, what we should do to prepare for it, and what we should do after it.

"Now you call me and you let me know how things are going once you have the blessing done." Talking to Ken was very easy. Suddenly we didn't feel so crazy, and we didn't feel so scared. Ken put us at ease, and we set out to find a priest.

36

It wasn't as easy as we thought it would be to go to a priest and tell him that Helen had demons in her house. Helen wasn't even remotely Catholic. She had been raised in a strict Baptist home, and she had a very hard time walking into the church that day. She could feel Jesus's eyes on her at every turn, staring at her from every painting and crucifix on the walls. Instead of finding comfort in Jesus, she found herself scared and slightly sickened at the thought of the crucifixion. Jesus wept, and Jesus made Helen uncomfortable.

The priest wasn't very old, maybe in his early forties. He sat at his desk with a picture of the pope on the wall behind him, the Holy Mother on another wall, and the eyes of Jesus staring at Helen from a crucifix on yet another wall. Helen felt as though she were on trial for her actions. *Jesus knows my secrets*. He knew that deep down she wanted to kill her husband and daughter. *He knows I want to kill them before they kill me.*

"Father," Helen began softly. "Father, my house is haunted." It was difficult for her to say those words to a stranger, and the shocked expression that crossed his face made her feel she had just made a dreadful mistake. He began to speak of the spirit and things along those lines. *Jesus is still staring at me. Oh God, his face is covered with blood.* The priest continued to talk, but Helen heard him through a haze. *Jesus knows my secrets.* Still the priest talked and the eyes of Jesus continued to bear down on Helen. Her hands began to fiddle on her lap.

"Father," she interrupted, "I need you to bless my house. Please. I can't stay here long. Tell me now. Will you do it or won't you?"

Startled by her intensity, the priest agreed, and an appointment was set. Satisfied, Helen excused herself from the room, from the church, and from the judgmental eyes of Christ. At that moment her thoughts were clear, and she tried to pray. *Our Father . . . who art in heaven . . .* Suddenly a horn blasted through her thinking as a car came screeching to a halt, coming very close to hitting Helen. She needed to watch where she was going. She forgot about continuing the prayer.

⁕ ⁕ ⁕

When the day of the blessing finally arrived, I got there early in case Helen needed bolstering. She appeared nervous, but she was in great spirits. The priest's blessing didn't take even five minutes; also, he didn't bless the house the way Ken had specified. In fact, the priest seemed profoundly nervous as we moved from room to room on the main floor.

"Father," I asked, "what about blessing the basement?"—whereupon he sprinkled a few drops of holy water down the steps.

"Father, what about the upstairs bedrooms?" Helen asked this time. The priest went to the top of the stairs and quickly sprinkled a few drops of water through each of the open bedroom doors. And then he was gone. He shoved a plaque into Helen's hands, gave us a quick "God bless," and he was gone.

The priest hadn't even reached his car before the banging began upstairs. Each boom seemed to confirm our fears that the blessing hadn't worked. It was the house telling us that it had been a joke, and once again Helen and I were left alone to deal with the problem.

Helen called Ken, who was sure that the priest had been frightened by the house. Ken suggested that we try to do the blessing on our own. What we didn't know at the time was that performing a blessing on a house is like pissing on a campfire—neither of these is enough to put out the flames. The demon was too close to us now, and it would take much more than one simple blessing to save us. And now the battle for our souls had begun.

37

Some days in your life you will always remember, days that for better or worse were different from all the days that preceded them. On these days you can feel the tide changing. You're not sure how or why, but you can feel that something significant has happened, or something significant is about to open.

It was Saturday, the day after the priest's half-assed blessing. Saturdays around the Union house were always busy with various groups coming and going. In that sense, this Saturday was no different.

Helen's morning began in its usual nightmare fashion. Kelly had a hamster that she simply loved. It was a poor little rodent that derived its joy in life from running on one of those squeaky wheels that people put in their hamsters' cages. This little thing could run as fast as it wanted to, but it was never going to get anywhere.

That morning Helen's attention was drawn to the cage because she didn't hear the wheel spinning. The hamster wasn't in the cage. Helen and Kelly had just started to search for it when Helen looked down at her feet. Lying on the floor was the hamster's skull. It had been picked clean and left behind to be found like some sick archaeological artifact. How had the hamster escaped its cage, and what could have done this to it in the middle of the night? Helen picked up the skull and discarded it with a shiver. Was this another response to the blessing from the day before? Helen wasn't sure, and she went about getting the house ready for the groups that would appear on her doorstep that day.

Among them were Bill and Trudy, a husband-and-wife team from a town south of St. Louis. From the moment I met them I felt there was something familiar about Trudy, as if I had met her before. And unlike most of the people who had trodden through the Union house, I was immediately comfortable with both of them. Later on, Trudy and I would figure out that not only had we grown up in the same neighborhood, but some thirty years earlier we had been in the same fifth-grade class! It was one of the strange outcomes of the Union house investigation that we would never be able to explain. We only knew that for some reason we had been drawn back together again.

Bill was a student of paranormal activity, and he was becoming quite good at capturing electronic voice phenomena, or EVP. He understood how to speak to a spirit in order to elicit a response. Anyone in his vicinity in the house quickly learned to be silent when Bill walked into a room, saying, "I'm holding a small gray box with a red light on it. If you were to try to speak into the box with the light, I might be able to understand some of what you'd like to tell me. What is your name?"

On this occasion he got a small girl saying, "The one." He continued, "Is there something you'd like to tell Trudy or me?"

With this, a woman's voice responded, "His point of view is distracted." Later, Bill found that if he reversed this EVP the woman could be heard saying, "Why don't you come and find me?"

EVP experts from around the country were becoming interested in the remarkable sessions Bill conducted at the Union house. It was thought that the reverse EVPs actually indicated areas of the house and land where a vortex could be found. We believed that we had located three. And that very night we were going to experience one of them fully.

Bill's wife, Trudy, spent most of her time at the Union house in silent concentration. She is a "sensitive" who can communicate with the spirits. Trudy grew up with the ability, always feeling in her youth that it was a curse. For a long time, Bill didn't fully understood his wife's gift, and to him at times it was just Trudy "being crazy." However, time and time again Trudy's instincts were correct and Bill began to listen to her.

Marie also arrived for the first time that night with her husband Evan. They were a happily married couple; Evan was the skeptic of the two, but within a few hours of entering the Union house and experiencing it for himself, he became a believer.

On the other hand, Marie, like Trudy, was a sensitive who had always believed in the paranormal world. One of her first experiences at the Union house was being pushed up the stairs. Later she saw a strange man walk into the bathroom; when she went to look for him, no one was there. And that night we were all in for something special, something new, and something that would help explain the Union house.

Helen and I had also invited a Christian women's group to attend that night's investigation. I'd decided that we would try to flush out the spirits by stationing people in every room of the house. Marie and Evan were posted upstairs. I stayed in the basement with Bill and Trudy. Helen was on the main floor with some other people. The Christian women were in the backyard.

Once everyone was stationed, the experiment started. One of the first things we noticed in the basement was that it began getting hot. The temperature quickly rose nearly twenty-five degrees. Trudy and I also felt the presence of something evil standing in the basement with us. It was laughing at us, mocking us, and we were both touched by something unseen. When we asked if the basement monster was with us, the EVP answer was "yes."

While the temperature was rising in the basement, the Christian women began to feel very uneasy in the backyard. The wind picked up, and they felt an electrical charge surge through the air. Something was going on that made them feel they weren't alone, and they went running back to the house. Later they said it was as though something was stalking them and then chasing them as they ran. One of the women was brave enough to pause and snap some digital photographs.

We could hear their noisy entrance from our post in the basement, and we went to see what had happened. The lady with the camera handed it to me to look. What she got on one of the photos shocked us all.

On the right side of the photo I could see an opening that seemed to flare with fire. It appeared that several entities had walked through that portal and gathered at the foot of something that was hard to make out in the fire. I could distinguish several faces, however. One was that of an old voodoo priestess who was looking straight into the camera, seemingly angry that we were interrupting their ritual.

After studying the photo for a few minutes, we could make out that they were gathered around a burning cross. Much to our horror we realized we were looking at the image of someone being crucified on that cross; we were looking at a mockery of Christ's crucifixion. A silence fell across the room. We now had proof that this was indeed a demonic haunting. And at that moment, although we were standing in a room full of people, Helen and I had never felt more alone.

38

Life seemed to go on normally for everyone else outside of the Union house. Sometimes I would look at others with normal lives and wish that my life could be more like theirs. My children were doing well. They seemed to understand the validity of what I was trying to accomplish. They understood that in some unseen way it wasn't just for Helen, but for all of us.

The children's lives went on with extreme normalcy. Of course, they often asked me questions about the house. Most of the time, though, I avoided the subjects that I thought I should avoid and was completely honest with the ones that I knew they could handle. It's very important never to lie to your children. Matthew would often ask me how Helen was doing. Helen, who felt a need for the son she had never had, quickly took Matthew under her wing and consistently spoiled him even through the worst of times. It was as though she instinctively knew that Matthew needed to feel comfortable with her in order to allow me to spend so much time with her.

I first made contact with John Zaffis in June 2005. By this time, I had seen many groups come and go. Helen and I had tried many different things, none of which seemed to work. After I made contact with him, I frequently talked to John on the phone. He would often just listen and offer advice. Never at any time did he make me feel I couldn't handle the situations ahead of me. Whenever I was at my last straw, I called John Zaffis.

John is a world-famous demonologist and paranormal investigator. He has over thirty years of experience and has worked on many famous haunting cases. If there were such a thing as being born to paranormal royalty, that would be John, who comes from a well-known line of researchers. However, John walked to his own beat and made his own way in the world. That's what I admire about him. And if he's reading this now, I'm sure he's saying, "Just shut up, Tiny"—he calls me Tiny—"and get on with the story."

When dealing with a haunted house, you find yourself encountering very puzzling things, which at first you aren't sure are paranormal or not. This was the case with the carpeting in the Union house. No matter how many times we shampooed it, large dark spots would appear a few days later. At times it seemed we could almost sit and watch the rug as it soiled itself. Crazy stuff.

One afternoon a few days after Helen had the carpet shampooed again, I was over at the house. "Steven, I just don't understand this. No matter how many times I clean this rug, it always looks like this a few days later. Do you know why?"

I sat there looking at the rug, trying to find some sane solution. But I knew that I couldn't, because I had made the same observation when I lived there. As a matter of fact, Mr. Winters charged me for carpet cleaning after we moved. Then I remembered hearing John talk about one of his cases, a poltergeist case in which it rained inside the house. And this rain stained everything it touched. At this point it seemed possible to me that the reverse was happening in the Union house. Maybe the water was coming from below and not above. So I suggested to Helen that we give John a call.

John answered almost on the first ring. We went through the normal pleasantries and then I told him about the carpet. "Well, you know where I come from we have a horrible time with mold. Do me a favor and pull back the carpet and tell me what you see," John said, sounding very interested. I handed the phone to Helen and told her to relay to John what I was seeing. She seemed a little dismayed when I told her I was going to pull up the rug. Now that I look back, it strikes me as funny. Anyway, I went to the corner of the room and I pulled back the rug to one of the worst spots on the whole floor. To my surprise, the rug looked completely brand-new underneath. Even the padding was fresh and clean. There were spots only on the top of the rug. Helen relayed this information to John, who had no explanation.

We never did figure out the mystery of the carpet, but something more important happened that day. Helen began to speak to John herself. And from that moment on I knew that if either of us needed him, he would be there to help and in some cases get us through the darkest days that lay ahead of both of us.

39

The Union house had become notorious for affecting people and their dreams. Certainly Helen and I had experienced many nightmares due to it. It was a nightmare that brought me back to the house in the first place, and nightmares were common occurrences for all of us who spent time at the Union house. None of us, however, could have been prepared for the second coming of Matthew's demonic clown and the many nightmares and problems it caused.

I hadn't spoken to anyone about the demonic clown for a very long time. I avoided the subject because I was afraid people would really think my son and I were crazy if I admitted that Matthew claimed he had been chased by an evil clown. In my own mind, I had been convinced that he used the clown as a metaphor for something that he was afraid to put a face on, or for something that he simply couldn't verbalize in any other way.

The clown's return was low-key at first. Helen had agreed to watch a friend's four-year-old daughter. Helen was holding the girl on her lap when the girl began to shake and then whimper. Slowly she raised her arm and pointed straight forward into the air. "Clown," the little girl said, "clown." Other than my immediate family, no one else knew about Matthew's clown. And when Helen told me this story later, she did so sheepishly. She was sure I would think she was crazy. Of course I didn't. But I was positive now that we were dealing with something that could read our fears and manifest itself as that which we feared most in order to shake us to our very foundations. At least that seemed like a logical explanation to me.

Naturally, none of us could have imagined that our friend and fellow investigator Marie had a phobia of clowns and that they had frightened her all her life. Clowns? Who would have guessed? But we were about to find out just how evil this demon clown could be, and it chose Marie to demonstrate its power and ability to frighten us, even torture us. What happened to Marie is hard for me to tell. It hurts me to think about it; it hurts me as I write this; and I'm afraid that it will hurt every time I touch on it. I feel responsible for the harm done to Marie's family, but how could I have known in advance how deeply this demon had infected the Union house or what a vicious predator it had become? It was preying on us, and we were still alone and helpless to deal with it.

One evening at the Union house, Marie was happily telling us that her nineteen-year-old daughter was expecting a baby. We were all quiet until she assured us that it was okay, and that she and Evan were actually excited to be blessed with their first grandchild. With this, we began heartily congratulating them. Within the coming week Marie's daughter would have her first appointment with the doctor.

The night before the appointment with the doctor, Marie woke up in the middle of the night screaming.

"I was standing in the side yard of the Union House," she said as she told me about her nightmare the next day. "I was standing in the side yard of the Union house. There were all of these people there, and they were just standing and staring up at the house. I remember joining them to see what they were looking at when I heard a giggle from behind me. It was deep and low, an evil giggle. I turned and there was a demonic clown with red glowing eyes behind me. He was holding a baby by its feet, and he was laughing. He had razor-sharp teeth that glowed in the moonlight. He laughed as he held the baby by its ankles and slammed it on the ground over and over again like it was a sack of potatoes. All the while the clown kept laughing and laughing. I screamed for people to turn around and help me get the baby away from him, but no one would. No one would turn. No one would move. It was as if something held them in a trance, staring at something on the roof that I couldn't see. I just kept screaming. Evan finally heard me screaming and woke me up."

Nothing could have prepared me for what she told me next. "We went to the doctor with my daughter this morning. They couldn't find a heartbeat. Steven, the baby is dead. They couldn't find its heartbeat." Marie began to cry.

I was at a loss for words. Did the house do this to her daughter? Was the nightmare a premonition, or did Marie's dream occur at the exact moment when the child lost its life in the womb of its mother? I hung up the phone. I was shaking, and then I, too, was crying.

40

Four a.m. What was I was hearing? Something was bringing me out of my sleep, sounding over and over again. The phone was ringing. Helen was at the other end, sobbing.

"Steven, I don't think I can take much more of this, Steven. I think something terrible is going to happen if we don't find a way to stop this thing." I did my best to settle her down.

"Tell me what happened, Helen. Tell me everything."

"Charlie and I went to bed at about ten. I was so tired. You know how tired I've been lately. I'm just so tired all of the time, so I went to bed early. I woke up to the sound of my own voice. It was my voice speaking, but what struck me was I was talking with no emotion. I was agreeing to something. I was saying something like, 'I can do that.' My eyes were still closed, but when I understood that it was my voice

I was hearing, I opened my eyes. Steven, there was a black-hooded figure sitting on my bed next to me. It was sitting there, and I was having
a conversation with it. When I comprehended what was happening, I
yelled and it disappeared. What do you think we were talking about?
What do you think I was agreeing to?" She began to sob again.

I had no idea what was going on. It took me until seven o'clock to
calm her down. We talked about everything we had been through as
we tried to make sense of it all. We asked each other yet again why all
of this was happening to us. The situation was deteriorating rapidly,
and soon events would occur that we couldn't have ever imagined.
The waking nightmare was preparing itself to begin.

41

Helen's husband, Charlie, had never been in much of a hurry to admit that he was living in a haunted house. When I first met him, I wondered how this guy could live in this house and not see it for what it was. In time I came to understand Charlie. I came to understand his mother and how he was raised. It wasn't that he didn't believe his house was haunted; it's just that he had decided long ago to try to coexist with the haunting. He used to say, "They leave me alone and I leave them alone." He also used to warn us, "If you go messing with this thing, you two are going to come across something that you are going to be sorry you came across." Every once in a while I would hear him talking to people at the house, and I would laugh at people's reactions to him. They were just not sure how to take him. He would say to them in the same breath, "My house isn't haunted, but

I've heard footsteps come walking down the stairs in the middle of the night, and I really don't care to go into that basement much." He had his own way of dealing with things, and I had to respect him for that. He would often say, "I don't have the time or the energy for all of this ghost stuff. I'm too busy trying to make sure the bills get paid. I just don't have time for anyone or anything else, living *or* dead." And that was very true because Charlie did work very hard.

His opinion changed completely one night when he woke up to see a dark-hooded, shadowy figure at the foot of the bed. "It was there. I couldn't believe what I was seeing, but it was there. It was like it was studying Helen and me as we slept, and it scared me. I couldn't speak. I couldn't move. You know it's easy to not believe in these things or to ignore them because you don't see them. Sure, I've heard the noises around this house, and sure I've felt like there was someone there when there shouldn't have been. But when you see it with your own eyes, now that makes things more real. Now that I've seen it, I'm not sure what I want done about it."

From then on, Charlie began to listen more closely to what was going on in the house.

On the same night that Helen woke up to find Charlie terrified and speechless, she had an experience of her own. "I went back to sleep after talking with Charlie awhile, trying to help him make sense of what he'd seen. I guess I'd been asleep for about an hour. I heard it at first—a low, deep growling. I opened my eyes and near the bedroom window I could make out an animal. It was wolf-like. However, it was like no animal I'd ever seen before. It just sat there growling. Then it opened its eyes. They were a strange shade of yellow and glowed. From the other corner of the room, I heard a voice and saw a shadowy figure shoot across the foot of the bed. I could clearly hear it moving, and then in a very low, very demonic voice it said, 'I'm here.' And then the wolf and the figure were both gone just that quickly. I knew they were really there because they left behind a foul odor that nearly gagged me.

"I got up to use the bathroom and splash some water on my face. On the way, I saw that Kelly was standing on the stairs. She wasn't moving; she was just staring at me. I asked what she was doing up and she said, 'Nothing.' She assured me that everything was fine. I said okay and told her to go back to bed. I didn't sleep any more that night. It was 3:15 in the morning and I was wide awake."

42

I could see we were quickly heading down a very dark road. The problem was that no matter what I tried, I couldn't find a way to get us onto a brighter path. By now I felt entirely helpless, for I was engaged in my own inner struggle. I knew what I had been experiencing for the last months. And if I believed that these horrible evil events had actually happened, weren't hallucinations or ugly nightmares, then I had to find a way to reconcile with God. If the evil Helen and I had experienced existed, then certainly it must be balanced by an equal portion of goodness. I see this in people all the time. Very few people want to acknowledge that if they believe in God, they must also accept that evil exists. They can rest easier at night if they don't think about the thin line they walk between the two equals. They also don't want to acknowledge that if we can experience the grace of God, then we must also accept that evil can cut across that same line at any moment. They don't want to hear that something like this could happen to them, to their children, to their friends. I'm here to tell you that this did happen to my family and me. It happened to Helen and her family. And it could happen to you. You have to think about the battle between good and evil to completely understand it.

I was invited to visit the chapel at the old Alexian Brothers Hospital in St. Louis. This hospital was the site of a famous exorcism case in the 1940s, the exorcism that broadly inspired the book and movie *The Exorcist*. The wing where the actual exorcism took place was torn down long ago. What most people don't know, however, is that the hospital chapel had connected the two wings together, and the chapel still stands, even though the old wing is gone. I will admit to being frightened as I reached for the door that led into the chapel. This is the same place they brought the boy who was undergoing the exorcism to pray. This is where they tried to get the boy to take communion. A huge battle for the soul of one young boy had been fought in this place.

Instead of being frightened, however, I felt a wonderful sense of overwhelming peace descend on me as I stood at the altar in the chapel. Then it hit me. I was standing in a place where the battle of good versus evil had been played out. Of course I would feel a sense of peace. I walked around outside, where the demolished wing once held its secrets. The sense of peace and calm that I felt in the chapel followed me. This is a place where good won its battle. Once I understood that, it became clear that those horrific events were irrelevant to the chapel today; it was a true house of holiness, peace, and serenity.

We should always remember the events of this hospital's past in order to avoid the evil attacks of the future. But more importantly, it would be grossly unfair to label either the Alexian Brothers Hospital or the chapel as places of evil. Remembering the past is fine, but ignoring the final outcome is foolish. How often can we say that about a place today? Thousands of people came and went through that hospital without much fanfare or applause. My own grandfather spent the last moments of his life there. How unfair it would be to let one incident overshadow years of kindness, tenderness, and mercy. As the old saying goes:

> *If you believe there is evil in your life, you will then see demons tear it apart piece by piece. But if you choose to see the beauty of your life, then you will see your life exalted by heavenly angels and your heart will be filled with the glory of God.*

It's all a matter of how you choose to view it. In the quiet meditation of that moment, I understood the beauty of the hospital and the power of its message for those who dared to open themselves up to it. And in that moment I felt hope for Helen and myself, hope and peace.

My hope was shattered that very night when I returned home. Helen called to tell me that she had been raped by an unseen force in the house. She had been asleep and woke up because she felt a tremendous pressure on her chest. She felt as though she couldn't breathe. Then she realized that she couldn't move. There was something large and heavy on top of her. To her horror, she realized she was being raped by the hooded figure that had been visiting her room night after night. She couldn't scream because she couldn't breathe. What bothered her most was that it wasn't a totally unpleasant experience. It wasn't pleasant that she was being held against her will or that she couldn't breathe, but along with all of that she had been sexually aroused, and that scared her more than anything.

43

We never mentioned the rape again. It was something we just didn't talk about. And for a long time Helen would rather have just completely forgotten it. She was raped three times by the demon that we know of. There could have been more rapes. Who knows? Rape is rape, and too often rapists get away with their crimes because their victims are mortified and unwilling to discuss it. A human rapist or demonic rapist, Helen's feelings were the same. I talked to John Zaffis on the phone more frequently. We both agreed that I needed to find a priest who would help, and I needed to find him fast.

It made it easier that the next night was Saturday. The usual crowd was once again gathered to try to make sense of this haunting. Everyone brought with them some advice on how to help us. The people and their advice made it easier for Helen to forget the rape and move on. We were surrounded by our friends—and no matter how bad things were, these were the times when we always felt the best.

Helen needed her friends that night. Earlier in the day she had told me she thought Charlie was having an affair. I asked her why she thought this. She said it was just a feeling, but she knew it. She could feel it deep down. Was it her guilt about the rapes playing out some strange scenario in her head? I wasn't sure. However, Helen continued to insist that he was having an affair, and she told me she was going to kill him when she found out for sure.

I could see the determination behind her words mirrored in her eyes. Later I would understand this look and understand what it meant. However, this was the first time I had seen that nasty glint in her eyes. It seemed to me that her eyes became very black when she mentioned killing her husband. Even her voice took on a slightly new tone when she spoke the words. A chill climbed up my back in that moment. Of course I couldn't believe that she meant what she said, that she could ever kill her husband. It was beyond my comprehension that this sweet, neighborhood mother and grandmother, my Helen who was always ready with a cup of coffee and a piece of cake, could kill anyone. I put her words out of my mind and helped her prepare for the Saturday night gathering.

The night went by fairly quietly. There were some marked cold spots. Some electromagnetic field (EMF) spikes. And Bill, as usual, had the most amazing electronic voice phenomena (EVP). There were a few cool pictures taken. But really, considering the Union house's history, nothing out of the ordinary occurred that night.

It was four a.m. when everyone left. Helen and I were sitting in the living room talking over cake and coffee. Suddenly, the whole room lit up bright blue from something outside. At first we thought it was another transformer blowing up outside or that it had been struck by lightning. Naturally, we ran to the front porch to see what had happened. What we saw was a black wolf standing in the middle of the street. It was blacker than black, if that's possible.

"There it is!" Helen said, pointing a shaking finger at it. "That's the animal that's been in my room at night."

With more energy than sense, I ran at it but it ran, too, across the street where it ducked into the alley. Foolishly I followed it, my prey, into the darkness. That's when the beast turned on me and I looked it in the face. There were the same glowing yellow eyes that Helen had seen. I could feel evil emanating from this creature. Unafraid of me, it stood its ground and growled at me. I fell to the ground as I stumbled away from it. I couldn't believe what I was seeing. Then, with one more growl, it ran away. Helen helped me to my feet, and we walked back to the front porch.

"Helen," I said quietly. "That was the thing you're seeing at the foot of your bed at night?"

"Yes, that's it," Helen whispered.

What in hell was this woman thinking? All of my pent-up emotions from the last months and years burst from me.

"Then, Helen, you've got to get the fuck out of this house. You need to move. Now! That wasn't a normal animal. That was a fucking devil dog sent from hell to grab your soul by the throat and bring it home. You're seeing this thing at night in your motherfucking room, and you aren't moving? It's time, Helen. It's time to get out now. You've got to move."

She didn't argue with me. I was clearly worried and frightened for her.

"You have to move." That was the end of the story as far as I was concerned. There would be no more attempts to find help for the house so Helen could continue living there. I needed to get her out and to safely immediately.

That was the beginning of Helen's last week in the house, but the start of many new nightmares for us both.

44

The week was fairly quiet. Sunday was quiet, too, except that I was exhausted. I had the kind of tired that hurts with deep muscle aches. I thought I might have caught a virus, so I spent the day in bed and didn't talk to anyone.

Monday came and went much the same way, although by now I could hardly lift my head off my pillow. I didn't dream; I experienced nothing but sweet merciful sleep. When I did wake up, though, I was more tired than I'd been before my last several hours of sleep. No matter how much sleep I got, my energy was being sapped faster than I could recharge myself; I have no clearer way to explain how I felt . . . I was just tired, exhausted, drained.

Tuesday was no different. The kids kept looking in on me, wondering what was going on, and I continued telling them that I thought

I had caught a virus. That night I tried to get up and watch TV with Lydia, but I found myself falling asleep in my chair. I even fell asleep in mid-sentence when I started to comment on the show we were watching.

After the show was over, I went to bed early. Again, sleep came very easily that evening and I didn't dream; I just slept. About six a.m., I heard a ringing that brought me back to reality. Through my grogginess I realized that the phone was ringing.

"Steven?" I was sure it was Helen, but something sounded different. "Steven, I think I'm going crazy. No, wait, I *am* going crazy. Every night I wake up right around three in the morning and every night the hooded shadow is sitting on the side of my bed. It's always the same. He's sitting there, and we're having a conversation. I don't know what we're talking about. I can't remember. And then I always see the glowing eyes of the wolf. As soon as I see the wolf, they're both gone." As she concluded, she began to cry.

"I'm losing it. I keep having bad thoughts, and I can't sleep without my door locked. When I forget to lock it, I wake up to see Kelly standing at the foot of our bed. She just stares at Charlie and me, and I feel like I need to protect us from her. If I don't, I'm afraid she may try to kill us."

It was becoming difficult for Helen to speak through her sobs, and I had to strain to hear her next words. "Steven, I think . . . I . . . could . . . kill . . . Kelly and Charlie both. I think I could. I'm afraid that if I don't kill them first that they will kill me. I know it's not just me. They're acting very strange too. I think someone is going to get hurt. I think . . . I think . . . someone might . . . die."

When she paused I tried to speak logically to her, to explain that in the middle of the night things often seem worse than they do in the daytime.

Suddenly, she cut me off and I noticed an immediate change in her voice. Her tone got lower and her speech became deliberate and concise. Her next words shocked me nearly as much as anything that had transpired up to this point.

"That motherfucker Charlie is fucking around on me."

My jaw fell open. I couldn't believe I was hearing this calm viciousness coming from the lips of this sweet woman, Helen, the grandmother! I had scarcely ever heard Helen curse, much less use language this coarse.

"Oh, I'm telling you, that motherfucking prick is fucking around on me. Oh, yeah. He's fucking that big-assed blonde he works with. I know her. I've seen him with her. She sometimes brings his ass home, and I know he's been fucking her. I can smell her cunt on him and it fucking stinks."

She fell silent.

"Helen? Helen, are you there? Helen?" Then quietly, almost meekly, she began to speak again. This time she was speaking like Helen. She started crying again. "What am I going to do? My whole life is falling apart. Where am I going to go?"

We talked deep into the morning. We talked about possibilities. We talked about futures. We talked about happiness and what it felt like to actually be happy and how that feeling had left both of us. Hour after hour we talked.

Around ten o'clock Helen abruptly said, "I have something I have to do. I'll call you later." And with that, she was gone. I sat on the couch thinking about all that we had said and everything that had transpired since I'd first met Helen a year and a half before. Finally, I got up and made a late breakfast and kept thinking. The phone rang and interrupted my thoughts.

"Steven?" It was Helen. This time she was eerily calm. Too calm considering her level of hysteria the last time I talked to her.

"I did something I shouldn't have done. I visited Charlie on his lunch hour."

I couldn't stop the next words that tumbled out of my mouth. "Helen, you didn't! I mean, Helen, you didn't hurt him, did you?"

She emitted a very wicked, very un-Helen-like chuckle. "I tried, but the son of a bitch got away."

"What are you saying, Helen? What did you do?" I tried to keep the panic out of my voice, but it was becoming more difficult by the second to keep myself calm and listen to her talk.

As if telling me about a visit to the grocery store, she calmly described her encounter with Charlie.

"I found the gun in the house. If thought if I was going to kill him anyway, I may as well get it done now. The cheating, fucking bastard. Yeah, might as well just get it done. I went looking for the clip, but I couldn't find it.

"You know what? Kelly had some friends over and none of them was acting right. They knew I was looking for the clip so I could kill Charlie, but they all stayed calm. It was really freaky. They even tried to help me find the clip so I could do it.

"After a while I gave up on finding the clip, and I decided to find something else. I thought about my walking stick, but that wouldn't work while he was awake. He'd see me coming and have the upper hand. No, unless I could come up with something else, I'd have to use the walking stick at night when he's asleep and then bash his head in, but yeah, he would have to be asleep if I used that. I didn't want to wait until tonight, though, so that ruled out the stick.

"What could I use? I tried the kitchen next, and Kelly's friends followed me in there. The little angels were so helpful trying to help me find the best way to kill Charlie.

"I decided to use the butcher knife. It was just sitting there on the kitchen counter. It's really sharp and I could use it to cut his throat, cut his throat like the fucking pig that he is. Then I would stab him in the stomach and I would cut off his dick and shove it in his mouth and watch him choke on it while he bled to death. That was it. It was simple, and it was perfect.

"Then one of the boys handed me a serrated-edge knife and said, 'No, use this one; it will cut easier and cause more damage quicker.'

"He spoke so calmly and with such assurance, and the rest of the kids agreed with him, so I knew he must be right. But I took both knives just to be on the safe side.

"It was weird the way they wanted to help me. They were acting very strangely. Shouldn't they have been trying to stop me? Then I realized they were just trying to help me and it was okay.

"It was funny, as I walked out the front door one of the little angels asked if he could watch me stab Charlie. I think it was the one who suggested the serrated knife. Anyway, I just ignored him and kept walking.

"I got into the car and put the two knives under the driver's seat so I could get to them easily until I needed one of them or both. The kids stood on the front porch, waving and watching me drive away. They looked like zombies standing there, like robots just standing on the porch waving.

"I felt great about what I was going to do as I drove. Charlie thought I was there to take him to lunch but, you know, I think he might have suspected something because he looked at me funny when he got in the car, like he wasn't sure it was me. He seemed nervous. I parked the car by the lake in the park, and I began to speak to him slowly, softly. There was no need for me to raise my voice because *I* had the fucking upper hand.

"'So, Charlie, you been fucking around on me?' It was fun; he even began to squirm a little in his seat. He said no, he hadn't been cheating. He even called me '*baby*,'" Helen said in a mocking voice. "I put one hand down by the side of the driver's seat. I could feel the butcher knife in my hand.

"I said, 'Don't lie to me, Charlie. Have you been fucking around on me?'

"'No, baby, of course not.'

"I put my hand back down so I could feel the butcher knife again. 'Don't lie to me, Charlie.'

"Ha! By now he was squirming so much I thought he was going to shit his pants.

"Then he said it one more time, he said he hadn't been messing around on me. This made me angry. I grabbed the knife. You should have seen the shock on his face and the way he was raising himself off the seat. I jabbed that knife at him over and over. Oh, I wanted to stab him in the crotch. And I kept saying, 'Don't you fucking lie to me! Don't you fucking lie to me, you goddamned son of a bitch.' And again and again I stabbed at him. I was trying to stab him in the dick, but he kept moving.

"Charlie reached for the door handle so I began stabbing at his hand. He wasn't going anywhere until he fucking told me the truth.

"Somehow he got the car door open and he was out and running back to work. I tried to hit him with the car, but I kept missing him so I stopped that. I knew I'd have another chance at him when he came home."

I couldn't believe what I was hearing. I had been right. Some-one was going to get hurt in that house, and to my utter shock it was Helen who would be doing the hurting.

"Helen," I said softly, "we need to get you out of that house and find you some help." I could hear Helen begin crying again. "Listen to me, Helen. Pack a bag. Put some clothes in it and your important things, the things you'd take with you if your house was on fire. I'll pick you up tomorrow at two in the afternoon, do you understand me?"

She agreed. She was very agreeable at this point. "Let Steven take care of it all" was going over and over in her mind. "Let Steven take care of it all."

It isn't unusual at this stage of an extreme haunting for para-noia to set in. Was Helen acting this way due to paranoia, or had the demons simply broken her down to the point of collapse? No one, not even Helen, will ever know for sure.

Later that night John Zaffis received a call from Helen. A call in which he would later claim Helen was off the scale, and he knew that things were about to get a lot worse.

Charlie didn't come home and Helen doesn't remember what happened to her that night. She woke up with bruises around her neck and bite marks on her back. This was worse than it had ever been before. And as she looked at herself in the mirror, Helen finally broke down.

45

The next morning I had to take Michael to the orthodontist. It was about noon before I got back home. The phone was ringing as I stepped onto the porch of my house. It was Helen. I could hardly understand what she was saying.

"It tried to kill me! It tried to kill me in my sleep! Steven, do you hear me? It tried to kill me in my sleep! I have these bruises, these bite marks. They're all over. All over! Help me, Steven! You have to help me!"

With those words, I was on the run. In the coming days when Marie would tell the story to those who would listen, she always began with, "God was with Steven that day."

After I left, the phone rang inside my house. It was John Zaffis, calling me to tell me he was extremely worried. I didn't get his call. I was already on my way to trouble.

Was God with me at that moment? Honestly, at that moment I didn't give God much thought. I just knew that I had to get to Helen.

Even in the light of day the Union house seemed ominous, alive. I could feel its electrical charge running through me as I parked the car.

Kelly was sitting on the hood of a car with two of her friends. I gave her a quick wave as I ran to the house, but none of them moved. I slowed down to look at them, and they were snarling. Dear God in heaven, these three children were snarling at me. I didn't bother knocking, I charged into the house. I found Helen in the living room. She was dressed and ready to go, and she was catatonic.

"Helen? Helen? C'mon, we have to get you . . ." The upstairs banging started right above us. "Helen, we have to get you out of here." She mumbled something as I held her by the arm with one hand, her packed bag in my other hand.

Boom! Boom! BOOM!

"Come on, Helen, we're getting you out of here!" When we got to the front door, I let go of her arm to open the door and on the other side stood Kelly, still snarling.

"Where are you going, bitch? Aren't you going to give me some money?" I stood our ground, Helen in front of me.

"Kelly, move."

Still snarling, she said, "Give me some money, you fucking bitch."

The booming continued overhead. "Kelly," I said, "move out of our fucking way!"

She stepped aside, and with my free hand I pushed Helen out the front door and rushed her to the car. The three kids were still outside, still snarling, still angry.

Once we got on the highway leading out of town, Helen began to speak, "Where are we going?"

"We're going to get you some help. We're getting you some help."

46

I took Helen to the emergency room at a hospital near St. Louis. At the time it seemed the only logical place to go. We were immediately met by a staff member and, after a moment, escorted into an examining room.

The nurse came in to perform the routine exams first. Helen's blood pressure was 209 over 198. The nurse shook her head and took it again with the same results. By all rights, Helen should have already had a stroke. Strangely, her pulse was at 40, which perplexed the ER doctors, and was dropping more by the minute. At this point, by all medical standards Helen should have been in a coma or dead. They needed to lower her blood pressure, but they had to do it without lowering her pulse.

The nurse looked at me. "You understand you saved her life?"

All I could do was utter a quiet "yes." Of course I understood I had saved her life, but Helen needed saving in more ways than they could understand.

The next person to see Helen was a jolly, heavyset fellow. "I'm going to ask you a few questions, and I want you to be totally honest when you answer them, okay?" Helen nodded her head in agreement. "Helen, do you have thoughts of hurting yourself?"

"Yes."

"Helen, do you have thoughts of hurting someone other than yourself?"

"Yes."

There it was. Helen was suicidal and homicidal, and the doctors knew it. There was no turning back now.

"Helen, would you like us to get you some help?"

Helen nodded in agreement and began to cry.

"Good. Dr. Smith will be your doctor, and I have to tell you that he is the best doctor around. So you're in luck."

Luck? Luck? He had to be kidding. Helen was being committed to a nut house—oh, excuse me, a behavioral health unit, and this doctor thought that today was her lucky day. Then I relented; maybe it *was* her lucky day.

Helen held my hand tightly as we walked down the hall toward the double doors where three security officers waited. They would escort her to the behavioral health building.

"Don't let go of my hand until they make you," Helen whispered to me softly as we walked toward the officers.

When we reached the door, one of the officers said, "Sir, this is where you need to say goodbye." I gave Helen a hug and turned her over to them.

As she stepped into the building she yelled after me, "Don't you forget me in here. Don't you dare forget me in here."

I raised my hand and waved goodbye without turning to look back at her. Tears ran down my face as I continued walking. I didn't want her to see me crying.

47

After I left Helen with the guards, memories of her began rushing through my mind. There was Helen smiling and laughing, the woman I had first met. But then there was the baby hanging in the tree . . . and Helen with a butcher knife in her hand—trembling, shaking, her eyes dilated, looking as if she were on acid. I reached the car and shivered as I got behind the wheel. I turned on the radio; I desperately needed company for the trip home, even if just a voice on the radio.

The only explanation I can give for what happened next is that God was sending me help, because the voice of John Zaffis started to come out of my radio.

"Yes, it rained inside the house," came John's cheerful voice through the radio, describing an investigation he had worked on.

I felt reassured as I listened to John answer the callers' questions. "God, I wish John could be here right now," I prayed aloud as I entered the traffic on the busy street.

This was a route I had driven for many years. Michael had been born in this hospital, and before that his mother had worked there. In the early days I would often pick her up, Lydia sleeping in her car seat in the back. The sleeping child always made for good company. At least back then I didn't feel alone. Not like that moment, when I felt very alone.

A truck stopped in front of me. Not a large truck, it was a mid-size moving van like the dinosaur van we always seemed to rent on our various moving days. For the first time that day, I smiled. Michael loved those dinosaurs. This truck didn't have any markings or exotic paintings on its side. It was just a pure white truck. We stopped at a light before turning onto the on-ramp to the highway.

The light turned green and traffic moved forward. The white truck was still in front of me as we began the climb to the highway. I looked down to check my speed and when I looked up, I screamed. I was no longer getting on the highway. I was *on* the highway. I was on the highway, and I was going the wrong way into oncoming traffic.

Drivers honked at me as they rushed by, swerving around me. I managed to get safely to the side of the road, and I waited until the traffic cleared so I could do a U-turn and face the right way with the traffic. What had I done? How had I gotten so turned around? I had driven this way so many times. And then it hit me for the first time: something was trying to kill me. Something was trying to stop me. Had I gone too far by taking Helen from the Union house? Was I now going to have to pay the price with my own life?

I was shaking as I pulled back into traffic. I took the next exit and stopped in the parking lot of a gas station. What was going on? Where had the truck gone to? What was I going to do? John's voice on the radio filtered through my thoughts. *God, I wish John was here.*

48

It was three in the morning when Helen woke up in her hospital room. It was the same time at which she'd been waking up for months. This time, though, she didn't wake up because of a sound, nor was anything sitting beside her on the bed. She woke up because she was cold. Her room was freezing. She got out of bed and put on a robe so she could walk down the hall to sit in the day room to warm up before going back to bed. She opened the door to her room and walked slowly down the hall. She was groggy from the sleeping medication they had given her, but she was aware of her surroundings and she was cautious. If she had learned anything in the last months, she had learned that this particular time of night could hold any number of horrific surprises for her.

As she walked, another patient stepped out of his room and stopped right in Helen's path. He was holding something in his hand, but Helen couldn't make out what it was until he started waving it above his head and yelling. He was holding a Bible.

"This woman is of the devil!" he cried, looking straight into Helen's eyes. "This woman is of the devil!"

White coats came running from all directions. They grabbed the man and tried to subdue him as he continued screaming. "This woman is damned! She is damned! Damned!"

Helen could still hear him screaming as the nurses dragged him back into his room. She kept her gaze forward as she passed his room. She didn't want to look at him, but she could hear him. "Damned! Damned! DAMNED!"

Helen was grateful when she finally made it to the day room. She just needed some peace and warmth. She closed her eyes and tried to erase the man from her mind. Then she heard the voice of another man from right beside her.

Helen opened her eyes to see him frantically thumbing through his Bible and begin reciting verses he had highlighted for her.

"Mark 5:15: 'And they come to Jesus, and see him that was possessed with the devil, and had the legion, sitting, and clothed, and in his right mind, and they were afraid.'" The man's hands frantically moved to find the next verse.

"1 Timothy 4:1: 'Now the Spirit speaketh expressly, that in the latter times some shall depart from the faith, giving heed to seducing spirits and doctrines of devils.'" Again, he frantically searched to find his next verse.

As he read the next one, he began to stroke Helen's hair.

"Revelation 18:2: 'And he cried mightily with a strong voice, saying, Babylon the great is fallen, is fallen, and is become the habitation of devils, and the hold of every foul spirit, and a cage of every unclean and hateful bird.'"

When he finished reading this verse, he began kissing her on the top of her head. *Oh my God*, Helen thought, *I'm under attack. I'm under attack!* Fortunately, a nurse walked into the day room and drew the man away. Helen heard the man repeating the word *evil* over and over as the nurse escorted him down the hall.

Helen went back to her room and sank into her bed, pulling the covers and pillow over her head to muffle the scream that was building inside her. The second man's words kept running through her head. Had she indeed become a "habitation of devils, the hold of every foul spirit, and a cage of every unclean and hateful bird"? That phrase rang over and over and over.

49

Imagine you're sitting in a waiting room and you've just told a stranger that you live in a haunted house where a black-hooded man and a wolf appear in your bedroom every morning at three a.m. You also tell the stranger you've been committed to a locked ward in a behavioral institution (let's get real, a mental institution) for evaluation because you tried to stab your husband to death. Maybe your tongue would be further loosened to reveal other stories about things that have happened to you and your friends at your haunted house. Would the person listening to you think that you were crazy or demonically possessed? It's hard to answer that question, isn't it? The typical person would probably listen politely for a few moments, nod at you, and wish you well as he or she looked for another place to sit. It wouldn't occur to this person that you might be completely sane.

This brings to mind the next questions: How many people who are considered insane are actually victims of the paranormal? Where does reality end and schizophrenia begin? These were the questions going through my mind. I was sure that Helen had to be wondering the same things. Could she be honest with her doctors and tell them exactly what was happening with her? Would anyone believe her? Or would her "true confession" just buy her more time in lockup? It was obvious from her first night's experience that the hospital wasn't going to offer her the safety we had originally thought.

"Did you tell the doctor about the house?" I asked her during one of our first telephone conversations.

"Not yet. Actually, I'm afraid to, but I know if I don't tell him, I can't expect to get the help I need," she replied in a very matter-of-fact way. To me this was one of those clear signs that she wasn't crazy, just the opposite; it told me that she was completely sane. She needed help and she knew she needed help. When a person is crazy, they don't realize they need help.

That was the first day. On the third day Helen was bursting with excitement over the phone. "I told my doctor that I live in a haunted house. I said to him, 'What would you think if I told you my house was haunted? Would you think I was crazy?' He looked me straight in the eye and said no. He wouldn't think I was crazy! Steven, he said he would help me. He said the only thing he could find wrong with me is minor depression."

Hallelujah, I thought. By the grace of God, Helen had finally found someone who could help her. She was so happy and excited that for a moment I felt I was talking to the old Helen. Then her tone changed. Her voice lowered. Her words became nonexpressive and deliberate. "Did you find a fucking priest yet?"

I was shocked. "Excuse me?"

She asked me again in the same deliberate tone of voice, "Have you found another fucking priest yet or do you think I have the time in here to find one? What's it going to fucking take! You can't find one simple fucking priest. That's all I want you to do, and you can't even get that done. I tell you what. I can do it by my fucking self. I can do it *all* by my fucking self." And the phone went dead.

At first I thought she had hung up on me. Later I learned that Helen, this tiny grandmother, had ripped the pay phone off the wall. "I had the strength of four men," she would claim while telling the story. An hour passed and my phone rang again. It was Helen, crying.

"Steven, I am so sorry. I'm under so much pressure. Of course I didn't mean any of that."

I told her that it was okay, that I understood. Then I told her that I had found a priest. A good priest named Father Paul. I just hadn't had a chance to tell her.

That evening, Carol from the MPR group went to see Helen. She called me later that night. "Steven, I think we've lost her. I really do. She just kept changing from one personality to the next. Her mood changed just as quickly. Her daughter was there, and she told me that she didn't know who that person was, but it wasn't her mother."

Helen was released from the hospital on Tuesday; we had an appointment to meet with Father Paul on Wednesday morning.

Father Paul came highly recommended by a friend who told me that he wasn't your average priest. "Father sees things."

I had to find out more. "What do you mean, 'Father sees things'? Are you saying he's psychic?"

Clearing her throat, my friend agreed. "Yes, if you want to call it that. Father is a psychic priest, but he prefers to call it *sensitive*."

Helen didn't return to the Union house. Dr. Smith and John Zaffis thought it best that we keep her completely away from the house. Helen went to live with her daughter in Gerald, Missouri, just a few towns down the road from Union. In the meantime, Charlie and Kelly were at the house picking up the pieces. Kelly underwent spiritual counseling and came around very quickly. Charlie found them a new place to live, and it was only a matter of time before they were out. Out of the house and out of danger.

50

I couldn't believe how good Helen looked when I picked her up for our appointment with Father Paul. She seemed a far cry from the crazy woman I had left at the hospital.

She remained quiet as we drove to the church, and when we pulled up in front of it, Helen commented on how pretty it was. And it was. It was an old, white, rock church sitting on top of a hill. Fall was upon us by now, and the land below us was a rich patchwork quilt of reds, oranges, and yellows.

Father's office was in a small house next to the church. He had lit a fire in the fireplace to ward off the autumn chill, which only added to the friendly environment we found ourselves in.

"Hello, I'm Father Paul," he greeted us, shaking our hands. He offered us seats on a large comfortable couch and pulled up a chair in front of us. "Please, sit," he said.

I remember thinking to myself, *So this is the great Father Paul I've heard so much about?* He had a very boyish face with warm features. It was a face you could talk to. He listened intently as we told him everything that had happened. I could almost see his mind working, contemplating, as he listened to us.

After listening to us carefully, Father explained that the house and the land surrounding it were the problem. Many bad things had happened there, and these events had opened the door to the demonic. "And," he added, "when you get one demon, you get many." He felt that I was suffering from demonic oppression and that Helen was suffering from an extreme oppression that was easily leading her down the road of possession. Then he asked if he could bless us.

"Close your eyes," he said to me as he lay his hand on top of my head and began to pray. I felt like I couldn't breathe. I felt as if I were having an asthma attack. *Oh my God, it's my dream, I can't breathe!* Then I became aware of a series of white flashes of light, very white, very quick. My breathing instantly settled, and I felt myself relax for the first time in months. Deep warmth rushed through me. The sound of Father's voice comforted me as he prayed, delivering me from evil with his prayer. When he was finished, I felt wonderful. I couldn't tell with Helen, but she said that she felt better. As I pulled into her daughter's driveway, she began to cry. "I think he might be able to help," she said.

I felt great on the drive back to Union, and I decided to visit my parents. Mom was home when I got there and noticed right away that there was something different about me. I told her about our visit to Father Paul. "Mom, I figured out a lot of stuff while I was telling the priest our story. I found some answers for myself."

I had been an easy victim for this thing because I was at the lowest spiritual point in my life. My wife had left me with the kids. My sister, Janice, had died. I was angry at God for that, for taking my sister away from me. I was so angry that I turned my back on God.

Mom listened intently, then leaned forward and put a comforting hand on my shoulder. "Steven, God didn't take Janice from us. God accepted her."

I looked at my mother with a new love and respect. My mother, who had lost her only daughter, was telling me it was okay. Her words meant everything in the world for me. God accepted Janice, and from that moment on, I understood.

51

Bill had never been a very religious man. Had someone asked, he would have said he was a total agnostic. By now, we had spent a lot of time together and we were brothers and partners in the paranormal field. I knew it was going to be a hard sell when I told him that I believed Helen was under demonic influence.

"There has to be some other logical reason, Steven. It's one thing to say that this haunting has affected her, but it's another whole can of worms if we come out and say Helen is possessed."

I could hear the shock in his voice. "Maybe not exactly possessed, but for sure demonically oppressed."

"I don't care what you want to call it. If it has 'demon' in it, no one is going to believe it."

Bill was right. If it ever got out that Helen was under demonic influence, there would be hell to pay when dealing with people. Of course, Bill was thinking into the future. That's one of the things that I love about him. He has a knack for thinking into the future while I deal with the present. He is truly my paranormal brother, always thinking about what is best for me. It pained him to see me hurting this way.

"Right now we don't have to tell anyone. But Bill, I'm telling you that there's something seriously wrong here." Bill agreed.

The MPR group, about twenty people, planned an outing for the weekend before Halloween, tied specifically to the holiday. We'd kicked around a lot of ideas before I suggested a local spot that has long been nicknamed Zombie Road. In my mind, Zombie Road was a perfect outing for Halloween. The whole concept of the outing was to celebrate the upcoming holiday. It was the perfect place.

Zombie Road is about five miles long. It's no longer used as a road and has been closed off. This meant we would be taking a two-mile hike through the woods in the dead of night. There was a railroad for children located at the end of the road. Its tracks ran the last mile of the hike. A very scenic ride, with the bluffs rising out of the darkness on one side and the moonlit river on the other. Bill, always thinking, had set it up with the head of the railroad for us to ride the small train the last mile of the road. Everything was set. We had gotten all the clearances we needed. We were headed to Zombie Road. Not one of us had a clue what we were about to walk into. We thought this would be a simple hike through the "hundred-acre wood," but in the end we were terribly wrong.

"Where are you going tonight?" Helen asked on the phone early that Saturday afternoon. I told her the plans for the group, never dreaming that she'd ask to go along.

"Can I go? I want to go. Sounds like fun."

At first I wanted to tell her no, but when I thought it about it I decided it might do her some good to get out. Besides, I didn't expect to come across anything on Zombie Road. I thought she might enjoy the relaxing walk and then the scenic train ride. I thought it might do her some good. Fresh air. Friends around her. Might be just what she needed.

Everyone was excited about the outing, talking about the hike and the cute little kiddie train we would ride on at the end of the hike. It was going to be a perfect night and a perfect outing.

It began to rain as we assembled for our hike. It was a steady, calm rain, but we weren't going to let it ruin our night. Besides, once we got under the tree canopy, the rain wasn't so bad.

As we walked, we paused occasionally to make sure the entire group was still together. At one stop I turned to talk to Bill, who was standing behind me. Right behind him was the white figure of a man wearing overalls. He was clearly a farmer from some distant past. He appeared to be listening with great interest as Bill spoke. And just like that, the man was gone. I couldn't believe what I had just seen, but I immediately understood that Zombie Road was going to be much more than a simple walk through the woods. Zombie Road was haunted.

All the while we were walking, I kept an eye on Helen, who seemed to enjoy being out and with friends. During the first part of the hike I could hear her laughing and talking.

Our next stop to gather the troops was just as eventful as the first one. This time we saw a shadow figure, blacker than black, rushing down a hill at us. Bill and I stood watching in awe, the railroad guy between us.

In a frightened voice, he asked, "What was that?"

I looked at him, a bit shaken, and said, "It was a shadow ghost."

The railroad man was now a believer. Someone in the group caught a photo of the shadow figure, and we took a few more minutes to look at it.

The farther we walked down the road, the creepier it became. What had begun as a simple hike was turning into a walk through haunted woods. There was something about that night I just can't explain. At times, we could feel eyes staring at us from the trees; we heard whispers. We saw things that we just knew we shouldn't have been able to see. Instead of a walk through the haunted forest in *The Wizard of Oz*, the night began to feel more like *The Blair Witch Project*.

I was very happy to see the train when we came around a corner in the road. It was a small train, but large enough for people to sit one to a seat. It was also a cold ride out through the bluffs and along the river. At some point I began to have an uneasy feeling that something wasn't right.

"Helen, are you there?" I called out. I heard her reply "yes" from the seat behind me on the train, and I breathed a sigh of relief.

When the train rolled into the station, it seemed as though everyone had enjoyed themselves. People were standing around talking and sharing their experiences. I approached Helen to walk back to the car with her.

"What the fuck do you want?" she said, glaring at me. I could feel her eyes on me in the dark, and I knew immediately I had to get her out of there.

"Let's go, Helen," I said as I grabbed her arm and began walking to the car.

"Let go of my fucking arm, you fucking freak."

I took a deep breath, and as calmly as I could, I said, "Come on, Helen. Get in the car." Reluctantly, she got in the car.

Bill walked over to where we were parked, and I rolled down the passenger window on Helen's side. He had noticed that something was wrong, and he wanted to make sure we were okay. He had just about gotten to the car when Helen lifted her head and looked straight at him, looked *through* him, and snarled. All Bill saw were her black, dead eyes glaring at him. "What the fuck do you want?" she growled at him.

Bill backed away from the car. "Nothing, Helen, nothing."

I told Bill I would call him the next day, and I began the long drive home.

Helen was quiet for most of the drive to her daughter's house. When she did speak, it was in erratic phrases and various moods. "You know I could kill myself on Monday, and you would forget me by Thursday." "Tell the people to stop looking at me as they drive by."

"Please don't let them see that I am dead." "You fucking idiot. What were you thinking, taking me out in the goddamn rain?" "Want to take me to see the fucking priest now?" I breathed a sigh of relief when I pulled into the driveway of her daughter's farm.

It was very dark that night, but I could make out the white house in the distance. The dogs rushed to the car to greet us, but they suddenly stopped and dashed away, whimpering as they ran.

"You fucking hate me, don't you? You think Helen has lost her fucking mind." Her voice became low and gravelly as she spoke. She glared at me in the dark, and even in the dark of the car I could see that her eyes were pitch black. I was seeing the dead eyes for myself. And I understood that I wasn't talking to Helen. I was talking to "It."

"I heard everyone talking about me tonight. I could hear them talking about that bitch Helen going crazy."

I could have tried to reason with her. Tried to tell her that no one had said anything like that, but I knew it was best just to listen. Looking out the window of the car, I became aware of black shadows rising up from the ground, moving toward the car and surrounding it.

I started the engine. I had to get us out of there. "Where the fuck do you think you're going?" She tried to grab the keys and turn off the car. She hit and scratched me while I pushed her over toward her side of the car. "Get the fuck out of here. I don't care. Leave. You got it fucking coming to you." She turned to face me, "You got it fucking coming to you . . ." She got out of the car and slammed the door. I left her standing in the dark, her laugh echoing in my ears, her black eyes burning into the back of my head as I drove away, laughing, yelling, taunting, "You got it fucking coming to you," as she stood amid the shadows.

I didn't slow down until I was well down the road and away from her. I slammed the steering wheel with a hand that shook uncontrollably. How could this happen? Why had this sweet, innocent lady been turned into this . . . this . . . monster?

Pulling into my driveway, I rushed into my house. My whole body was still shaking, and I was as frightened as I have ever been in my life. The phone rang just as I stepped inside. It was Bill. He was worried about what he had witnessed when Helen and I left. He had seen into the eyes of evil, too. We both now understood what we were dealing with.

52

It was well past dawn before I finally fell into a strange, restless sleep. It was late in the afternoon when the phone rang. One of the kids picked it up, and Matthew came bounding into my room with the phone in his hand. "Dad, it's Helen's daughter."

My heart sank into my chest. I just knew that she was calling me to tell me that Helen had killed herself. I had a horrible feeling that something was about to happen, a feeling I couldn't shake.

"Steven, I'm sorry to bother you, but my mom has been acting very strange all day. She stormed out of the house a few hours ago and drove away. I don't know where she is."

I tried to calm her down. "Tell me what happened."

"It started this morning when I took her to church with us. She sat in the pew during the entire service. One minute she was crying, and the next minute she was angry. She said to me at one point, 'Why did you bring me to this church, you fucking bitch?' I tried to quiet her down. But I couldn't. She either had tears running down her face or she was saying the most horrible things. I don't know who that was, Steven, but that wasn't my mother."

Again, I tried to calm her down, this time succeeding in a very small way. I told her what had happened the night before. I told her everything.

Then she began to speak again, "When we got home from church, she was very wound up. She was screaming and yelling at me. Then, before I knew it, she went racing out of the driveway. Steven, I am so scared. What are we going to do? We have to find her help."

At this point I almost said, "To hell with 'we,' what are *you* going to do?" But Helen's daughter sounded so desperate. How could I turn my back on her? How could I turn my back on Helen? I agreed that we would find help.

Later that night I got a call from the daughter, saying that Helen had come home and was acting completely normal, as if nothing out of the ordinary had ever happened. When she arrived she went straight to bed because she said she was just "so gosh darn tired."

I was glad to hear that Helen was finally home. And I tried to decide what our next step would be. What could we do? The next day was Halloween, and we had all agreed to enjoy the day with our children. We would figure this out the day after Halloween.

53

It was Halloween 2005. I had always loved Halloween. The kids and I always tried to do something special on Halloween, and this year would be no different. The kids were going trick-or-treating at dusk, and then would come home to watch a few scary DVDs. Matthew, as he was on most holidays, was up at the crack of dawn. I could hear him and Michael in the next room making plans for scaring little kids that night. Michael was excited because he had bought the newest in zombie makeup, prosthetics and all. "And tons of fake blood," he added gleefully. The kids were clearly excited. It was seven-thirty in the morning before I finally got all three of them on the bus.

I sat down on the couch with a big sigh. I smoked, thinking about the day ahead, trying to forget the events of the weekend past. I put out my cigarette and began to fall asleep. My cat Zelda snuggled by my side, purring. My other cat, Athena, stood guard over us from the back of the couch. The warmth of the cat and her purring put me to sleep.

At eight-thirty there was a loud knock at my door. Whoever was out there was knocking so hard that the noise shook me wide awake. The banging came again. It sounded like my "visitor" wanted to break through my door. I looked out the side window; it was Helen pounding at my door. She knew that I had seen her because she looked right at me, her eyes black as night as she snarled, "Steven, let me fucking in. Steven, I mean it. Let me the fuck in." She held something behind her back, but I couldn't see what it was.

Again, she pounded on the door, yelling, "Steven! You son of a bitch! Let me fucking in." Her fists hammered harder than ever and she kept yelling. I headed to the door. I had to get her inside before she woke up the entire neighborhood. Her pounding increased in intensity even as I went to the door. As I got there, something made me look at my feet. Both of my cats were there. It was as if they were trying to block my way; they were arching their backs and hissing at the door. A split second before I put my hand on the handle something went through my mind, something about paying attention to animal behavior. And in that moment I knew I had better not open the door.

"Steven, let me in, you fucking cunt-ass motherfucker." Her voice was low, loud, growling. "Let me fucking in, you son of a bitch." It seemed like it went on forever. I was picking up the phone to call the police when I heard Helen's car squeal out of the driveway. I dialed her daughter instead. "Listen, your mother was just here, and she was out of her mind. I thought I was going to have to call the police on her."

Helen's daughter said she would try to reach Helen on her cell phone and would call me right back. "Sit tight," she said. "I'm at work and it might take a minute." The phone rang about five minutes later.

"Listen, Steven, if she comes back there, do not open your door. Do you hear me? Do *not* open your door!! She has a gun, and she's sitting outside of the Union house. She says that if I call the police, she'll be dead before they get to her. Steven, it didn't sound like her. Look, I'm on my way. Do you think you can try to talk to her on the phone and stall her until I get there?"

Still in shock, I reluctantly agreed. "Good. Steven, pray for me. The girls at work here are already praying. Pray for me and pray for yourself, but whatever you do, do not open your door to her."

I sat on the couch and took a deep breath. So it had come to this. This was where it had all been leading. This was the moment of truth. I had to talk Helen out of suicide. I had to talk her out of it right after she had come to my home to kill me. I took another deep breath and dialed her number. She picked up almost immediately.

"What do you want, you goddamn son of a bitch? Want me to go to the fucking priest again?"

I had to stall her. I had to try to reach her through whatever it was that I was talking to now.

"You know what I'm doing right now, you fucking prick? You want to know? I'm holding a fucking gun to my head. It would be so easy to pull the trigger and just blow my fucking head away. What would you tell the fucking priest then?"

Trying to maintain my composure, I said, "I would tell him that I had just lost my closest friend."

She laughed. "I'm not your fucking friend. Never have and never will be. Want to know what I have planned next?"

I tried to reason with her. "Tell you what. Why don't you put down the gun and then tell me what you want to do."

Surprising me, she said, "Okay." A second later I heard the glove compartment in the car shut. "The gun is put away. I wasn't going to use it on myself anyway. Now you, you were a different fucking story. Fucking coward. Wouldn't even open the door for a little old lady. Fucking prick."

I needed to get her back on track. "What are you planning to do now?"

She laughed. "I'm going to hang myself in the basement of that goddamn house. Yeah. I'm going to let the motherfucker have me. Break the basement window and hang myself in the butcher shower."

An immediate chill raced through my veins. This wasn't Helen.

She once told me that her biggest fear was that she might die by choking to death. She couldn't even wear a tight necklace around her neck. As I remembered that, I realized anew that I wasn't talking to Helen.

Through the phone I heard a knock on the car window and the voice of Helen's daughter. Helen hissed at me. "What is that fucking bitch doing here? Did you fucking call her, you prick?"

Calmly, I said, "No, Helen, you did."

I heard a change in her voice. "What?"

"Yes, you called her, Helen. Don't you remember?"

The only way to explain what I heard next is to say that I heard a long, sorrowful howl come over the phone. It started low and began to build. I could hear shock and confusion in her voice when she finally spoke again. "I called her? Wait a minute. What in the hell am I doing here? Steven, what am I doing in front of this house?"

"Helen, answer a question for me. I already know the answer, but I want to make sure you know what I'm talking about. How long have these blackouts been going on?"

There was a moment of silence and then she admitted, "Since last Christmas."

"How often do they happen and for how long?"

Her answer shocked me. "Some weeks are better than others. At first it was just an hour or two here and there. Lately, I've been losing days."

"Mom? Mom?" I could hear her daughter begging Helen to let her in at the window.

"Helen, I want you to take a good look at your daughter's face. Look at her. See the pain you are putting your family through. Look at the pain in her eyes. Can you see it?"

Crying, "Yes, yes, I see it."

"Good, then you understand that we need to get you help."

With that, Helen opened the door and let her daughter in the car. After a moment her daughter's voice came on the phone. "I'm taking her back to the hospital. She wants to be sure that you call Father

Paul." With this last statement I knew that I had gotten through to her, to Helen. Thank God I got through to her.

Looking at my cats, I silently thanked them for saving my life. Later Helen would tell me that the demon had come to her and told her that she was going to kill me and then hang herself in the basement. That was all she remembered until she came to in the car that Halloween morning. If I had opened my door, both Helen and I would now be dead. The demon would have won. I do believe with my whole heart that God was with me that day.

It took many hours of therapy with Dr. Smith and many sessions with Father Paul to get Helen back to where she is today. Hours of advice from and talk with John Zaffis helped me heal the wounds of the experience and the results of the many mistakes I made. The road has been long and has not been easy. During Helen's recovery, John Zaffis told her, "You have a long haul ahead of you. This thing will not let you go that easily. This is a battle you are going to fight for years to come."

And John was right. It has been nothing short of a battle, a battle for both of our souls. You see, we all have a door. For most people this door is safely locked and never opened. For those whose doors do open, they will find that the doors can be closed but never again will they be securely locked. Yes, once unlocked, they may as well be swinging doors. This is the way it is for those of us who battle the dark side, who are engaged in spiritual warfare. And remember that's exactly what it is: spiritual warfare.

54

Those early days of recovery were hard ones, not just for Helen but for me as well. In the quiet of the days that followed, I understood that I, too, had a lot of healing to do. My very first reaction was to completely leave everything associated with the paranormal behind me, to forget it and turn my back on those whom I might be able to help. It was self-preservation. I told Bill and Trudy that I was closing down MPR and leaving it all behind. They had also been changed by everything that had transpired, and they wisely told me to go and take some time to heal. They would hold the group together for as long as it took, because someday I was going to get better, and I was going to come back. I was going to come home.

I began attending church again. For the first time in years I took communion, and as I did I cried. How had I gotten so lost? I don't really know, but it had been disturbingly easy. My daughter gave me a key chain that I carry with my keys today. It was a reminder from when I was a little boy, and on the key chain is a poem I loved then and I cherish now:

Footprints in the Sand[1]

One night I dreamed I was
walking along the beach with the Lord.
Many scenes from my life flashed across the sky.
In each scene I noticed footprints in the sand.
Sometimes there were two sets of footprints,
other times there was one only.
This bothered me because I noticed that during
the low periods of my life,
when I was suffering from anguish,
sorrow, or defeat, I could see only one set of footprints,
so I said to the Lord, "You promised me, Lord,
that if I followed you, you would walk with me always.
But I have noticed that during the most trying periods of my life
there has only been one set of footprints in the sand.
Why, when I have needed you most,
have you not been there for me?"
The Lord replied, "The times when you have seen
only one set of footprints, my child, is when I carried you."

* * *

In the beginning, one of the first things Helen had asked of me was that I stay with her until we saw this thing through to its conclusion. In her mind, Helen always felt that once we were done with the Union house our friendship would be lost. I promised her I would be there until the end and remain with her after. Many people have come and

---

1. There is a dispute about the authorship of "Footprints in the Sand." This version, said to date from the late 1930s, is often attributed to Mary Stevenson (1922–1999).

gone throughout the years of the Union investigation, but my friendship with Helen has held fast through the good times and the bad. When someone else would come and go, she would look at me and say, "Hey, you're still here."

My response was always the same, "Of course I am. I promised."

One of the many amazing things about Helen is that she fully understands that we lived through something that very few people have survived. She was always willing to open her house to this group or that group, this person or that person. Very rarely did she ever tell someone that they couldn't come in. Time and time again, as groups came and went, people would tell me that Helen always made them feel at home.

"I want them to be able to learn from this house," she would tell me. "And I want them to feel at home."

One day in the car coming home from the hospital, Helen asked, "What do we do now?"

What do we do now? I thought about it and then I answered, "Helen, you and I stood on the edge of something greater than we are or ever will be. What we do now is put our lives back together and start living again."

"How do we do that?" she asked me gently, tears in her eyes.

"One day at a time, that's how we do it. One day at a time. Together."

All of this time I thought that it was me helping Helen, but in the end it was Helen helping me, saving me.

During one of our visits with Father Paul, he and I were walking out of the church together when he asked me how the paranormal investigation team was doing.

"Oh, Father, I left that behind me."

He put his hand on my back and said, "Maybe you should reconsider that? Maybe you've been given this second chance to help others?"

His words resonated within me, and that night I picked up the phone to call Bill. "I'm ready," I told him. I was ready to go back to my team and to help people again. Father Paul was right. I had been given a second chance, and second chances should never be thrown away.

I remember John Zaffis saying to me, "Steven, if you walk away now after waging this battle, the demons will come at you sevenfold."

John made Bill promise him that he would never let me do that. John Zaffis used to tell me that this isn't a path that anyone would choose for themselves. It's a path that is chosen for them. Once on the path, it is impossible to leave it. I understand now what he meant.

55

Two years later . . .

How can you sum up in a few words a healing process that took years? But day after day, month after month, year after year, the healing process continues, both for Helen and for me.

Of course there are lingering signs that we went through something pretty horrific. For example, I hate crowds. I am very nervous when I'm in a large group of people. I am not paranoid, I am cautious. If you didn't know me or know about my wounds from the whole nightmare Union house experience, you might not even notice that every once in awhile I will look to my right, my left, behind me. Looking for that moment when the demon will find a way to get to me through a sickened person who has gotten too close to me. And I do mean "sickened," because I look at this as a disease, a cancer on the face of humanity. That's some heavy shit, is it not?

My faith in God has never been stronger. My faith guides me in my journey to help others afflicted with this demonic disease. My faith is what gets me through some of the darkest hours. What are the darkest hours, you might ask? Standing in the middle of an old man's house watching him fall apart as all of his life belongings come crashing down around us. That was one of the darkest hours. Trying to help a woman who wakes up every morning with mysterious bruising on her inner thighs and bite marks on her back. Those were dark hours. So was listening to a five-year-old child as she tells me that her doll is telling her to kill her four-month-old brother.

How do you deal with this kind of pain and misery, let alone attempt to help these good people? Through faith. Only a person of faith can take away the pain of the demonically afflicted. On a radio show I was asked if I am a demonologist. First, I have never been the kind of person to get into labels. No, I'm not a demonologist. Then the answer came to me. It came to me clearly and concisely, and I gave my response without reservation. "I am a man of faith who helps those in need." That is what I do and that is who I am.

Helen's recovery was slow. It took numerous visits to the priest and the psychiatrist. Sometimes it seemed she was never going to recover, and I would never get her back. Relapses were commonplace in the early days as she fought her way back. What should never have become routine became strangely appropriate. Off to the hospital, then to the priest, always in the same order: Hospital, priest. Never did we vary from this odd little routine for it worked well and we knew it.

For the first two years, Helen was highly medicated. At times I couldn't understand what all the medication was for. As it was, I did eventually understand that Helen needed the medication to heal as she coped with her feelings and her pain.

Was Helen demonically possessed? There are those who would tell you that she was, without a doubt. However, John Zaffis did not agree with full possession with regards to Helen. John believes that a full possession needs an exorcism. Yet there are others who believe that sometimes exorcism is too extreme, and you can actually hurt the possessed person more or even kill him or her through exorcism.

What do I believe? I know what I lived through and I know what I saw and heard. I have looked into the eyes of evil, and I have survived some horrible, frightening events. I tend to leave the labels for the experts. I don't need to debate terminology to understand the magnitude of what I survived and what I saw Helen survive. Oppression or possession? Who cares? I'm just glad to be alive.

Word has spread about my demonic fights at the Union house and people are calling me, seeking help either for themselves or for a family member or friend who is experiencing their own extreme haunting. Some cases I can solve with a simple phone call and some reassurance, but other cases will take months, even years, to bring to resolution. I can't desert those who come to me for help. It's a battle between good and evil, you see. And I fight it one case, one soul at a time, with the help and continued guidance of my friends.

Epilogue

Three-bedroom house for rent in Union. Full in-town living. Near most schools and the city park. Perfect for families. A full country kitchen with up-to-date amenities. Large living and dining area with original woodwork intact. Two bathrooms with mudroom. Full basement with fruit cellar attached. Large front porch and backyard perfect for children. The right house at the right price for the right family. If interested, please contact . . .

The ad for the house ran in the newspaper in December 2005, the same ad that had been used to lure me in and was used to lure in Helen. In fact, it seemed to me that it had most likely been used many times before. Whatever the case, it was very clear that old Mr. Winters was looking for a new family. Not long after reading the ad in the newspaper, to my surprise I got an e-mail from Mr. Winters, telling me that indeed a new family had moved in to the house, a family with young children. Mr. Winters celebrated having new young victims in the house. He reveled in it:

> *The new children are having fun running around upstairs and "screaming" as children do when they're having fun . . . but I bet the parents will stop that soon, when they finish moving in and get unpacked. When the kids first got there, they immediately ran up the stairs, as little tykes do. They began running in and out of the rooms, screaming and laughing with joy . . . It was so nice to hear "little angels screaming" . . . I hope their guardian angels will watch over them.*

Little angels screaming. With that said, he didn't need to say anymore. I had my answer. The one remaining question that I had about the whole experience was answered with those three words: *little . . . angels . . . screaming.* Was this Mr. Winters' way of mocking me? Celebrating his victory? The question was answered. I believe that not only did Mr. Winters know what was going on in the house, he was feeding it families. Fresh meat for the lion hiding in the cage, and his favorite was the children.

Photo by Tim Clifton

About the Authors

Steven LaChance (Missouri) is a radio host and producer who appears weekly on *Haunted Survivor Radio*, an online radio program. His story was featured on the Discovery Channel's *A Haunting* and in the Booth Brothers documentary *The Possessed*. He also appears in *Children of the Grave*, another documentary by the Booth Brothers.

Steven's experiences at the Union house inspired him to form the Missouri Paranormal Research Society, which he left in 2007 in order to help people in extreme haunting situations. He has successfully investigated and concluded many such cases. Steven speaks at paranormal conferences, and is traveling across the United States with the Haunted Survivors Tour.

Please visit Steven's website at www.stevenlachance.com.

Laura Long-Helbig (Missouri) is an English instructor.

Free Magazine

Read unique articles by Llewellyn authors, recommendations by experts, and information on new releases. To receive a free copy of Llewellyn's consumer magazine, *New Worlds of Mind & Spirit,* simply call 1-877-NEW-WRLD or visit our website at www.llewellyn.com and click on *New Worlds.*

LLEWELLYN ORDERING INFORMATION

Order Online:
Visit our website at www.llewellyn.com, select your books, and order them on our secure server.

Order by Phone:
- Call toll-free within the U.S. at 1-877-NEW-WRLD (1-877-639-9753). Call toll-free within Canada at 1-866-NEW-WRLD (1-866-639-9753)
- We accept VISA, MasterCard, and American Express

Order by Mail:
Send the full price of your order (MN residents add 7% sales tax) in U.S. funds, plus postage & handling to:

Llewellyn Worldwide
2143 Wooddale Drive, Dept. 978-0-7387-1357-1
Woodbury, MN 55125-2989, U.S.A.

Postage & Handling:
Standard (U.S., Mexico, & Canada). If your order is:
$24.99 and under, add $3.00
$25.00 and over, FREE STANDARD SHIPPING

AK, HI, PR: $15.00 for one book plus $1.00 for each additional book.

International Orders (airmail only):
$16.00 for one book plus $3.00 for each additional book

Orders are processed within 2 business days.
Please allow for normal shipping time. Postage and handling rates subject to change.

Ghosts, Apparitions and Poltergeists
An Exploration of the Supernatural through History

BRIAN RIGHI

The perfect manual for the ghost enthusiast, aspiring ghost hunter, or anyone who likes spine-tingling true tales, this book has something for everyone! It looks at the stories behind famous ghosts through history, ghost hunting and the original ghostbusters, mediums, spirit communication, spirits, apparitions, poltergeists, and more. This ghoulish guide is unique because it blends the history of the paranormal and paranormal investigations (including some infamous cases) with the ghost stories that accompany them. It can be read as either a handbook for ghost hunters or as a collection of true scary tales for pure enjoyment.

From ancient Babylon to nineteenth-century séance chambers to modern-day ghost hunts, paranormal investigator Brian Righi takes the reader on a fascinating exploration of the supernatural. Readers will venture into creepy moonlit cemeteries, ghost ships, and haunted castles, learn how to conduct a ghost hunt of their own, and spend time with some of the greatest ghost hunters ever to walk through a haunted house.

978-0-7387-1363-2
264 pages

$15.95

To order, call 1-877-NEW-WRLD
Prices subject to change without notice

The House of Spirits and Whispers
The True Story of a Haunted House

ANNIE WILDER

Annie Wilder suspected the funky hundred-year-old house was haunted when she saw it for the first time. But nothing could have prepared her for the mischievous and downright scary antics that take place once she, her two children, and her cats move into the rundown Victorian home. Disembodied conversations, pounding walls, glowing orbs, and mysterious whispers soon escalate into full-fledged ghostly visits—provoking sheer terror that, over time, transforms into curiosity. Determined to make peace with her spirit guests, she invites renowned clairvoyant Echo Bodine over and learns fascinating details about each of the entities residing there.

Wilder's gripping tale provides a compelling glimpse into the otherworldly nature of the lonely spirits, protective forces, phantom pets, and departed loved ones that occupy her remarkable home.

Annie Wilder is a mother and writer. Bravely, she continues to live in her spooky old house with three cats and numerous ghosts. This is her first book.

978-0-7387-0777-8

192 pages $12.95

Also available in Spanish

To order, call 1-877-NEW-WRLD
Prices subject to change without notice

True Hauntings

Spirits with a Purpose

HAZEL M. DENNING, PH.D.

Do spirits feel and think? Does death automatically promote them to a paradise—or, as some believe, a hell? Real-life ghostbuster Dr. Hazel M. Denning reveals the answers through case histories of the friendly and hostile earthbound spirits she has encountered. Learn the reasons spirits remain entrapped in the vibrational force field of the earth: fear of going to the other side, desire to protect surviving loved ones, and revenge. Dr. Denning also shares fascinating case histories involving spirit possession, psychic attack, mediumship, and spirit guides. Find out why spirits haunt us in *True Hauntings*, the only book of its kind written from the perspective of the spirits themselves.

978-1-56718-218-7

240 pages $12.95

To order, call 1-877-NEW-WRLD

Prices subject to change without notice

The Ghosts on 87th Lane

A True Story

M. L. Woelm

After moving her young family into their first house—a small suburban home in the Midwest—a series of strange and chilling events takes place: unexplained noises, objects disappearing, lights going out by themselves, phantom footsteps. And then M. L. Woelm's neighbor confirms the horrifying truth: her house is haunted.

Beginning in 1968 and spanning three decades, this moving memoir chronicles the hair-raising episodes that nearly drove an ordinary housewife and mother to the breaking point. With friends who thought she was crazy and a skeptical, unsupportive husband who worked nights, the author was left all alone in her terror. How did she cope with disembodied sobs, eerie feelings of being watched, mysterious scratches appearing on her throat, and a phantom child's voice crying "Mommy!" in her ear?

Discover how frazzled nerves and constant stress wreaked havoc on the author's health and marriage, until she finally found validation and understanding from a ghost expert, as well as from her friends, her grown children, and finally . . . her husband.

978-0-7387-1031-0
288 pages

$12.95

True Tales of Ghostly Encounters
COMPILED AND EDITED BY
ANDREW HONIGMAN

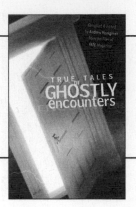

FATE magazine has published thousands of ghost stories, the true experiences of ordinary people who have had extraordinary encounters with the hereafter. Compiled and edited by Andrew Honigman, this collection features the best of these chilling, bizarre, and heartwarming tales. These detailed accounts of messages, gifts, blessings, and assistance from the spirit world provide remarkable proof of life after death.

978-0-7387-0989-5
312 pages $13.95

To order, call 1-877-NEW-WRLD
Prices subject to change without notice

Ghost Worlds

A Guide to Poltergeists, Portals, Ecto-mist & Spirit Behavior

MELBA GOODWYN

From communicating with spirits to witnessing orbs bursting from an inter-dimensional portal, Melba Goodwyn has seen it all as a psychic spirit investi-gator. In this fascinating examination of paranormal phenomena, she offers original insights into the nature of ghosts and haunting, true stories of her thrilling adventures, and practical ghost-hunting tips.

How are traditional ghosts different from poltergeists? How does a place or an object become haunted? What are orbs, ecto-mist, vortexes, and energy anomalies? Goodwyn defines different kinds of ghosts and entities, and explains how they manifest and why they are attracted to certain places.

978-0-7387-1195-9
264 pages

$14.95